PRAISE FO
(TC

MW00989513

"A fine book: lively, clear, accessible, but also deep, and deeply competent."

—*Alvin Plantinga, Emeritus Professor of Philosophy at the University of Notre Dame, author of* Where the Conflict Really Lies: Science, Religion, and Naturalism, *Oxford University Press*

"The Bible identifies Jesus as the Word and as the Light, available therefore to the mind as well as the heart. Of all religions, Christianity most invites one to think as well as to believe, and in this troubled time that invitation is still more urgent to take up. Here is a book by a skilled thinker, showing how better to think about faith. It is a worthy task, ably achieved."

—*Larry P. Arnn, PhD, president, Hillsdale College*

"This book is what snarky atheists have coming to them for their dismissive claims and unfounded arrogance. Written not to convince atheists but to help Christians defend themselves and the Christian faith, *A Shot of Faith to the Head* takes the best tools of top-notch apologetics and philosophy and puts them in the hands of every believer. Even better, it's easy and fun to read, winsome, witty, filled with sharp thinking, and well-researched. As a professor and pastor, I'll be assigning this book in my apologetics courses and would recommend it to every Christian. It displays strategic answers to questions and objections every Christian has encountered."

—*Justin Holcomb, pastor, Mars Hill Church; executive director of the Resurgence; adjunct professor of theology, Reformed Theological Seminary*

"*A Shot of Faith to the Head* is much more than a defense of Christianity; it takes the offensive against the secularist thinking that presently enamors so many in the West. Mitch Stokes demonstrates the intellectually dubious nature of the so-called 'new atheism' and provides Christians with a much needed handbook for the questions they will surely face. I highly recommend it."

—*Larry Taunton, president, Fixed Point Foundation; author of* The Grace Effect

"There is a cultural movement afoot that is irrational, atavistic, dogmatic and dangerous—I speak of course, of the new atheists. Mitch Stokes is the antidote. *A Shot of Faith to the Head* is a wonderful book: theologically sound, relentless in its reason, and fun to read."

—*Mark Judge, journalist and author of* A Tremor of Bliss

A SHOT OF FAITH

{TO THE HEAD}

Be a Confident Believer in an
Age of Cranky Atheists

MITCH STOKES, PhD

THOMAS NELSON
Since 1798

NASHVILLE   DALLAS   MEXICO CITY   RIO DE JANEIRO

To Shane, Summer, Jared, and Elena.

Published in Nashville, Tennessee, by Thomas Nelson. Thomas Nelson is a registered trademark of Thomas Nelson, Inc.

Thomas Nelson, Inc., titles may be purchased in bulk for educational, business, fund-raising, or sales promotional use. For information, please e-mail SpecialMarkets@ThomasNelson.com.

Library of Congress Control Number: 2012931126

ISBN: 978-1-5955-54345

Printed in the United States of America

13 14 15 16 QG 6 5 4 3 2

CONTENTS

PART 2: "SCIENCE HAS SHOWN THERE'S NO GOD"

PART 3: "EVIL AND SUFFERING SHOW THERE'S NO GOD"

PREFACE

'm just glad *I* believe."

It was about the worst answer she could have given me. Her reply not only revealed her frustration, but also suggested she was giving up—that I was to be left alone with my doubts. And what really bothered me was that it started looking like my questions had no good answers, which just confirmed my suspicions.

Maybe science was responsible for my doubts. Engineering had trained me to demand a special kind of evidence for my beliefs—*scientific* evidence. This vague requirement extended to all my beliefs (I thought), even to my "religious" ones. And to be sure, a thread running through this book is the alleged conflict between science and belief in God and the related allegation that science has shown that God doesn't exist.

I've since learned that science was indeed responsible for my doubts, but in a surprisingly different way. For years I had been immersed in a discipline that altogether ignores questions of philosophy and theology (and history and literature and anything else not covered by physics, chemistry, or mathematics). My education and vocation had been restricted and lopsided. It was as if I had lifted heavy weights with only my right arm, allowing the rest of my body to atrophy. Science without good philosophy—as you'll learn in this book—distorts and stunts our growth. At its best, unaided science results in idiot savants.

Whatever the cause(s) of my own doubting, I found that people had already addressed many of my questions. Some of these people had died centuries ago; others had years left. A few of them only made things worse, but many had good answers. All in all, I was rehabilitated. My belief in God stood.

But I still respect the questions. I even entertain them, putting them in their proper place. Questions are natural, and ignoring them is unnecessary and even dangerous. Addressing them, on the other hand, usually yields sizeable dividends.

I eventually left a comfortable and promising engineering career, returning to graduate school, this time in philosophy. I found myself surrounded by some of the best philosophers in the world, many of whom were serious Christians.

Christian philosophers? Yes, and it's one of academia's most closely guarded secrets. For the last four or five decades, these philosophers—who are enthusiastic about science—have developed powerful intellectual weapons, ones proven in the war between faith and unbelief. Many of these are alarmingly simple. Learning them is like turning an inverted picture right side up: anyone can do it, yet it makes everything look different. Everything finally fits.

These weapons are immensely helpful and it's time you knew about them. You need them. I daresay every believer does. The stakes are about as high as they get.

INTRODUCTION

SMARTER THAN THOU

Some local atheists recently rented a billboard near my home. The sign's message contrasts the things Christians "believe" with those that atheists "think." Christians, apparently, believe in God *without* thinking; they *just* believe. The idea is as clear as it is common: religious believers embrace irrationality, in contrast to the atheist's careful employment of cool reason.

This charge is a damning one too. In the West, as far as virtues go, rationality ranks just above love and only slightly beneath attractiveness. To be irrational is to be intellectually substandard, maybe even mentally defective. And by association, this is also what it is to have faith, to believe in God. Atheist Sam Harris, in his bestseller *The End of Faith*, offers this diagnosis:

> We have names for people who have many beliefs for which there is no rational justification. When their beliefs are extremely common we call them "religious"; otherwise, they are likely to be called "mad," "psychotic," or "delusional."[1]

Simply calling insanity "religion," says Harris, doesn't make it any less insane, just as calling a horse's tail a "leg" doesn't make it any less a tail (as Abraham Lincoln is said to have pointed out). If Harris is right, being religious is even worse than being unattractive. And that's bad indeed.

But why do Harris and his unbelieving cohorts think that Christians are irrational simply by dint of believing in God? For atheists, belief in God is irrational because it lacks the requisite *evidence*. According to the physicist Victor Stenger, "Faith is always foolish and leads to many evils of society. . . . Faith is belief in the absence of supportive evidence." Science, meanwhile, "is belief in the presence of supportive evidence. And reason is just the procedure by which humans ensure that their conclusions are consistent with the theory that produced them and with the data that test those conclusions."[2] Faith—and therefore religion—differs from reason and science in an important way: faith is belief based on no foundation, supported by nothing but wishful thinking. Science, however, traffics only in logic and cold, hard facts.

That atheists mention science and reason in the same trembling breath is to be expected, as we'll see. But for now, we need only note that science is seen as reason incarnate, the highest manifestation of man's rational capacity. Following this estimation, popular atheist Christopher Hitchens—who passed away in late 2011—lent praise to "a small but growing group of devoted rationalists, who reject the absurd and wicked claims of the religious and who look for answers in the marvels and complexities of science."[3]

The alleged absurdity of belief in God, coupled with the glories of scientific rationality, helps explain the atheists' frequent condescension and smarter-than-thou posturing. Richard Dawkins, the distinguished Oxford biologist and atheist, contrasts his learned ilk with the believing bumpkins in the United States: "What is remarkable is the polar opposition between the religiosity of the American public at large and the atheism of the intellectual elite."[4]

Philosopher Daniel Dennett even publicly campaigned to have himself and other atheists called "brights." Here he is in the *New York Times*:

The time has come for us brights to come out of the closet. What is a bright? A bright is a person with a naturalist as opposed to a supernaturalist world view. We brights don't believe in ghosts or elves or the Easter Bunny—or God. We disagree about many things, and hold a variety of views about morality, politics and the meaning of life, but we share a disbelief in black magic—and life after death.[5]

Not surprisingly, Dawkins joined the brights campaign.[6] But Hitchens, to his credit, called the whole thing "cringe-making."[7] Other adjectives also come to mind.

"Humble" isn't one of them. Yet the biologist Massimo Pigliucci says that science is "a much more humble enterprise than any religion or other ideology."[8] Of course, belief in your own humility undermines said belief. The sentence "I'm humble" is always false.

THE (ANTI) CHURCH MILITANT

The atheists' complaints against religion aren't merely academic. As they see it, the believer's lack of intellectual responsibility is more than a matter of ideas; it is a thing of immense practical concern. Our irrationality, they say, makes us dangerous, not merely dolts. Naturally, this troubles the atheists, whose militant leaders—Hitchens, Harris, Dennett, Dawkins, and Stenger—see religious belief as something to eliminate rather than merely ridicule. "We must find our way to a time when faith, without evidence, disgraces anyone who would claim it," writes Harris. "Given the present state of our world, there appears to be no other future worth wanting."[9]

Of course, religious people *can* be dangerous. Most of us think of September 11, 2001, when Muslim extremists flew airliners into the World Trade Center towers and the Pentagon, killing thousands. We're all aware of *this* kind of danger. Yet extremists aren't the sole threat. The perils of religion surround us daily. According to Dawkins, you or your parents (or both) have probably committed horrific crimes in the name of God. In his article "Religion's Real Child Abuse," Dawkins approvingly quotes psychologist Nicholas Humphrey:

> Freedom of speech is too precious a freedom to be meddled with. . . . Children, I'll argue, have a human right not to have their minds crippled by exposure to other people's bad ideas— no matter *who* these other people are. Parents, correspondingly, have no god-given license to enculturate their children in whatever ways they personally choose: no right to limit the horizons of their children's knowledge, to bring them up in an atmosphere of dogma and superstition, or to insist they follow the straight and narrow paths of their own faith. In short, children have a right not to have their minds addled by nonsense.

Ominously, Humphrey adds:

> And we as a society have a duty to protect them from it.[10]

Dawkins thinks that a religious upbringing is *worse* than most forms of child abuse. Once asked about the Catholic priest sex-abuse scandal, Dawkins actually said that "the damage [from molestation] was arguably less than the long-term psychological damage inflicted by bringing the child up Catholic in the first place."[11] The only thing more lacking than his sensitivity is his sense of perspective. Rape or religion? Dawkins says it's arguably worse to teach children that Christianity is true than it is to violate them sexually.

If these atheists are being genuine—and I have no real reason to doubt their sincerity—they're trying to set the stakes very high. There's a certain amount of bluster and theatrics of course; nevertheless, in their offer to protect our children from religious teaching, it's hard not to detect more than a whiff of good old-fashioned totalitarianism. Christopher Hitchens's brother, Peter Hitchens, a Christian, says that after Lenin's coup, schools were immediately secularized, religious teaching having been forbidden by Anatoly Lunacharsky's education decree on October 26, 1917, one of the very first broadly political acts of the Lenin putsch. There was then a second, still more devastating decree (on January 3, 1922), which utterly banned the teaching of religion to children, even singly, in churches, church buildings, or private homes. . . . "Collective teaching and isolated relations with young people under the age of eighteen, no matter where carried on, will be prosecuted with all the rigour of revolutionary law." Such "rigour" could include the death penalty.[12]

If religious education amounts to literal child abuse, it's difficult to see how Dawkins and Humphrey could find such measures disagreeable.

Whatever the tactics, a cultural war is afoot. Only struggle will produce the secular future that Harris and others envision. To get there, said Christopher Hitchens, "We have first to transcend our prehistory, and escape the gnarled hands which reach out to drag us back to the catacombs and the reeking altars and the guilty pleasures of subjection and abjection. . . . To clear the mind for this project, it has become necessary to know the enemy, and to prepare to fight it."[13] Hitchens said elsewhere that one of the few things he and the late William F. Buckley Jr. agreed on was that "the duel between Christianity and atheism is the most important in the world."[14] Both sides can at least agree on the situation's gravity.

PHILOSOPHY'S RELIGIOUS REVOLUTION

While atheists have been deriding the idiocy of believers, the number of professional Christian intellectuals has been on the rise. Indeed, since the late 1960s, a revolution has occurred in academic philosophy. By 1980, the revolution was large enough to attract the attention of *Time* magazine. *Time*'s article "Modernizing the Case for God" begins with the tag, "Philosophers refurbish the tools of reason to sharpen arguments for theism." The article then announces,

> God? Wasn't he chased out of heaven by Marx, banished to the unconscious by Freud and announced by Nietzsche to be deceased? Did not Darwin drive him out of the empirical world? Well, not entirely. In a quiet revolution in thought and argument that hardly anyone could have foreseen only two decades ago, God is making a comeback. Most intriguingly, this is happening not among theologians or ordinary believers—most of whom never accepted for a moment that he was in any serious trouble—but in the crisp, intellectual circles of academic philosophers, where the consensus had long banished the Almighty from fruitful discourse.[15]

Only sixteen years earlier, *Time* had run the cover story "Is God Dead?" At that time, it took a considerable effort to catch sight of a Christian in philosophy departments. The precious few remaining kept their religious heads down. The reason? Atheists had convinced nearly everyone that religious language was utter gibberish, having no linguistic meaning at all.

This idea gained purchase because of excellent marketing. A school of philosophers called the "logical positivists" (*positivism* here means empirical or observable) had claimed that science, mathematics, and logic reveal that religious talk is akin to Lewis Carroll's delightfully silly "Jabberwocky" (minus the delight):[16]

> *'Twas brillig, and the slithy toves*
> *Did gyre and gimble in the wabe:*
> *All mimsy were the borogoves,*
> *And the mome raths outgrabe.*

These sentences look meaningful—they at least appear to have a decent grammatical structure. Nevertheless, they're complete nonsense, not even having the decency to be false.

But why think that religious language is anything at all like "Jabberwocky"? This verdict was handed down by the logical positivist's standard for what kinds of sentences are meaningful. According to their measure of meaningfulness, there are only two kinds of legitimate sentences: (1) those that are about things we can *observe*—like the sentences of science coincidentally—and (2) those that are true *by definition*—like the sentences of mathematics and logic (again, surely a coincidence). The first criterion corresponds to the *positivist* part of "logical positivism," the second to the *logical* part.

But we can't use observation to determine whether sentences about God are true; nor are they true by definition. The conclusion then is easy to see, as is the problem it posed for Christian philosophers. Offering arguments for God's existence would be like trying to argue that the slithy toves really did gyre and gimble in the wabe. A whimsical project at best.

But philosophers eventually saw that the very sentence expressing the logical positivist's standard of meaningfulness (that is, the sentence, "There are only two kinds of meaningful sentences: (1) . . . (2) . . .") failed to meet its own standards, and the logical positivists' project imploded in spectacular fashion. It hasn't been seen since.

The fall of logical positivism in the 1960s created breathing room for Christian philosophers. Without the draconian criterion of logical positivism, atheists could no longer dismiss out-of-hand sentences expressing religious belief. These sentences were back to being either true or false, and philosophers could once again argue about God's existence. It was like old times.

One of the first philosophers to take advantage of this resurgence of the old-time philosophy—and undoubtedly the most important—was a young Protestant philosopher, Alvin Plantinga. Plantinga had helped bring logical positivism's reign to a close, and, using the advanced tools of logic and analysis, turned his philosophical attention to the rationality of religious belief.

It wasn't that Plantinga was looking for reasons to believe in God. He already believed. Rather, he was devoting his philosophical efforts to a particularly Christian understanding of things—something like St. Anselm's *fides quaerens intellectum*, "faith seeking understanding." That is, rather than *arguing for* God's existence, Plantinga took belief in God as his starting point. If the atheists weren't interested in such a project, so what? And if they were scandalized, that was probably a good sign.

Since then, Plantinga has led the revolution in Christian philosophy (the 1980 *Time* article called him "America's leading orthodox Protestant philosopher of God"[17]) and in the process has become one of the most highly respected philosophers of any persuasion. In addition to his accomplishments in the philosophy of religion, he has made significant contributions to mainstream metaphysics, epistemology, and modal logic.

Many Christian philosophers have entered the academy along the way, and a considerable number of them are the best and brightest philosophy has to offer. Some of the vanguards include Plantinga's close friend Nicholas Wolterstorff, professor emeritus at Yale (the two attended Calvin College together, both as undergraduates and as faculty), Richard Swinburne, George Mavrodes, the late William Alston, and many more besides. The ranks continue to swell; in fact, the Society of Christian Philosophers, founded in the late 1970s, is "the largest single-interest group among American philosophers."[18]

The current situation, I think, has a distinct aesthetic appeal. On the one hand, we have atheists decrying religion's pathetic irrationality, and on the other, some of the best thinkers alive displaying just the opposite. We have new atheists and new theists, a pleasing symmetry.

THE DEVIL INSIDE

Of course, to some degree, the war between belief and unbelief exists in microcosm inside every believer. We should remember, as Plantinga says, that "believers are constantly beset by doubts, disquietude, spiritual difficulty, and turmoil . . . It never goes that well with us, and it often goes a good deal worse. There is an unbeliever within the breast of every Christian."[19]

Often, however, the cause of our doubt isn't what you might think. It isn't necessarily the *strength* of the arguments that rattles us, but the way they resonate with the unbeliever in each of us (what the Bible calls the "old self"[20]). We hear Tokyo Rose's voice and she seems to make pretty good sense sometimes. Yet more often than not, if we look closely at the atheist's arguments, we find that there is little substance. Seeing this can change the argument's frequency and therefore break its spell.

Believers often worry that their doubts signify the rapid approach of full-blown unbelief. But as pastor and author Tim Keller puts it,

> Faith without some doubts is like a human body without any antibodies in it. People who blithely go through life too busy or indifferent to ask hard questions about why they believe as they do will find themselves defenseless against either the experience of tragedy or the probing questions of a smart skeptic.[21]

All thoughtful believers—even those whose faith is mature—encounter doubt. Not a single person has had unadulterated faith.

In any case, it certainly won't do to ignore your doubts, and defusing them will only strengthen your faith. To be sure, doubts can be strong enough to become a trial in your life; but like all trials, they're meant to refine faith, not stifle it.

A NECESSARY SHOT TO THE HEAD

As I said in the preface, the purpose of this book is to take a few of the most important intellectual weapons, tactics, and strategies from recent Christian philosophy and put them in your hands. These are, in my estimation, the main things you need to know, providing excellent results with minimal effort. But they're not mere luxuries. Without these resources, we'll lose the current battle, leaving it for our children and grandchildren to fight. That's not an option I care to entertain.

Notice that the goal here isn't to convince atheists to believe in God; it's to train you to handily defend yourself. Yet sometimes the best defense is a good offense. I'll cover that too.

You will see that reading the new atheists—like reading the old—can actually be a welcome shot of faith, at least after some coaching, which this book provides. Ultimately, the result of the atheists' campaign may unpleasantly surprise them. But my guess is that their recent efforts—and growing shrillness—are the result of having already seen it coming.

But this result won't occur by itself. Believers must be armed with answers—for themselves as much as for those who don't believe. Again, the book you hold in your hands covers what I think are the most important topics in the debate between Christianity and atheism. The answers it provides aren't simply intellectual niceties, areas of interest to only philosophers or academics. Rather they're strategic answers to questions and objections we've all encountered.

Here is how we'll proceed. In Part 1, we'll look at the most fundamental objection to belief in God, namely that religious belief is irrational because of the utter lack of evidence for God's existence. This is the most fundamental objection because any response to it sets the stage for all further discussion. A wrong answer to the objection will end in disaster, and most Christians *have* given the wrong answer. To adequately respond to this objection, we'll need to look at the nature of evidence, along with the related topics of faith, reason, and arguments. The upshot will be that your belief in God can be rational even if you have no arguments for God's existence. In fact, the result will be stronger than that: we'll see that if belief in God always requires evidence or arguments in order to be rational, then atheism is irrational.

After dealing with the first objection to belief in God, we'll see that—even if arguments aren't necessary for believing in God at first—arguments may become necessary to defend your belief in God (and for other reasons). So in Parts 2 and 3 we'll deal with two powerful objections to the existence of God—objections that may just be as powerful and common as the first objection. Before addressing the arguments associated with these objections, we'll take an important intermission to learn some lessons in the art of intellectual self-defense: arguing. In this self-defense section we'll learn such things as just how much we should realistically expect from arguments, who has the burden of proof (and when), and what sorts of things we must and must not put up with when arguing with unbelievers. But, even in the process of learning how to defend ourselves, we'll accumulate reasons to think that arguments against God's existence are tenuous. Once these lessons are learned you'll be equipped to handle arguments in ways you never thought possible.

After the Intermission, we'll move to Part 2 and the ubiquitous claim that science has shown that God doesn't exist. This claim is supported in a myriad number of ways, and we'll address the most important ones. In the end, we'll see that, if anything, science gives us powerful reasons to believe in a divine designer.

Part 3 deals with what is perhaps the oldest of all objections to belief in God: that the existence of evil and suffering show that he doesn't exist. This is sometimes called the "Achilles' heel" of Christianity and raises thornier issues than do the previous objections. Not only that, the intellectual force of this objection is buttressed by a strong emotional or psychological component, making the argument seem more cogent than it actually is.

In the concluding chapter we'll see how Parts 1, 2, and 3 are tied together in a way that strongly suggests that atheism is completely undone.

FOR YOUR ARSENAL

- The new strain of atheists are no longer content to merely argue that God doesn't exist. They also claim that belief in God is dangerous and must therefore be eliminated.

- After decades of retreat during the early twentieth century, Christian philosophers have emerged to become the largest single constituent of academic philosophy.

- The weapons and strategies developed during the recent revolution in Christian philosophy can provide ordinary believers with powerful answers to the current crop of militant atheists.

PART 1

"Belief in God Is Irrational"

PART 1

"Behold Our God Is Emotional"

"NOT ENOUGH EVIDENCE, GOD!"

CHOOSING MY RELIGION

There is little to no evidence for God, and so Christians are forced to take what refuge they can in a feeble, sometimes fleeting faith. Eventually there will be no place left to hide.

This idea—false though it is—has worked its way so deeply into our culture, and is so intractable, that we need to pull it up by its roots. We find these roots in the eighteenth-century European Enlightenment, an intellectual and cultural movement that fell hard on the heels of the Scientific Revolution that caused it. There was a great rejoicing among many European intellectuals. Those living in darkness saw a great light, they believed, a light that would drive back the supposed darkness of religious ignorance and superstition. The light was science—or reason actually, which makes science possible.

Three of the most important Enlightenment thinkers shared a single muse: the English scientist Isaac Newton. Voltaire, David

Hume, and Immanuel Kant all believed that Newton had shown that reason (through science) is the key to understanding reality. And they were right to be impressed. Newton's mathematical science revealed many of the universe's secrets.

But notice that mathematics is something we do entirely with our minds. There's no need to check the world—no need to count—to see whether 16,478 plus 3,943 really does equal 20,421. We know it by reason alone. Of course, reason is linked to nature by our senses, by our observations. Even mathematical physical laws must agree with what we see. But observation is often merely the way we check or confirm the mathematics; it's the mathematical order beneath the observations that we're ultimately after. And so reason is primary; it holds the keys to the cosmos.

Blinded and disoriented by the brilliance of Newtonian science, many thinkers chased the light itself, rather than the things it revealed. One of the Enlightenment's more rambunctious episodes was the French Revolution, where in an antireligious frenzy, the revolutionaries converted Christian churches to temples of Reason. They replaced one religion with another. This is more silly than surprising; after all, the question isn't *whether* you will worship but *what*. Not coincidentally, Christopher Hitchens ended his book *God Is Not Great* with the chapter "The Need for a New Enlightenment." Who am I to stop him? Freedom of religion is the American way.

A REASONABLE REQUIREMENT

During the Enlightenment, then, reason became the arbiter, judging even religious beliefs. From this time on, says Nicholas Wolterstorff, a believer must hold "his religious convictions on the basis of other beliefs of his which give to those convictions adequate evidential support."[1] Like any belief, belief in God must be supported by sufficient evidence. In fact, this requirement applied to all beliefs and was the Enlightenment's standard for rationality:

To be rational, a belief must be supported by sufficient evidence.

This standard is important enough to be named—it's the same standard of today's atheists. Let's call it *evidentialism*.

Now is as good a time as any to point out that, so far, we really have only a "gut feeling" for what counts as evidence. To be sure, we know that evidentialism requires that all beliefs be supported by evidence, whatever evidence turns out to be. But with no clear criterion for what counts as evidence, we can't actually determine whether a belief has any. We'll find that nearly everything of substance hinges on this. For now, however, simply go with your gut while we focus on other things first. There will be time enough to nail down precisely what evidence is. You'll find it very instructive to see *how* the fog clears as we proceed.

Notice that evidentialism isn't contrary to religious belief *per se*, not as long as the belief in question rests on sufficient evidence. According to evidentialism, belief in God—indeed, any belief—is fine as long as there's evidence for it. Nearly all Christians have agreed: if religious beliefs don't conform to the standards of reason, we should reject them. Indeed the origin of evidentialism—at least the first to express it clearly—was a Christian: the English philosopher John Locke.[2] Locke, a close friend of Newton's, was concerned about a group that claimed it had received new revelation from God. These believers were known as "enthusiasts," a derogatory term meaning, roughly, "religious nuts." To avoid "anything goes" in religion, said Locke, we need some way to curb this enthusiasm. Religious pluralism—the existence of conflicting religious beliefs—requires a method for discerning the rational from the ridiculous. Locke insisted that we follow evidentialism. Any rational religious belief will be supported by sufficient evidence. We have adhered to this standard ever since.[3]

What could be more reasonable?

NOT UP TO CODE

Locke believed that Christianity met the evidentialist requirement, which he set out to show in *The Reasonableness of Christianity, As*

Delivered in the Scriptures.[4] But though nearly everyone agreed with Locke's evidentialism, not everyone shared his optimism about whether belief in God could meet it. According to a growing number of rationalist thinkers, Christianity didn't pay proper homage to reason. And if reason no longer sanctioned traditional religion, then neither would reason's disciples. The exodus away from Christianity began.

So we now have two claims. The first is evidentialism, the view that rational beliefs require sufficient evidence. Here's the second:

> *Belief in God is not supported by sufficient*
> *evidence and therefore is not rational.*

Let us call this second claim the evidentialist objection to belief in God, or simply the *evidentialist objection*. The evidentialist objection obviously depends on evidentialism, but a Christian could accept the requirement for evidence without for a moment conceding that belief in God doesn't meet this requirement. Again, evidentialism doesn't preclude adequate evidence for God. In fact, part of the reason Christians enthusiastically endorsed evidentialism was their confidence in the evidence. And so the arguments came rushing in.

GOING MEDIEVAL FOR A MOMENT

But were arguments for God's existence something new? Weren't Christians already giving such arguments long before the Enlightenment's evidentialist objection? What about the entire medieval tradition of natural theology, where philosophers offered arguments that depended not on Scripture, but on reason alone? During the Middle Ages, men like Anselm of Canterbury and Thomas Aquinas took arguments for God's existence to new levels of sophistication. Weren't they trying to show that belief in God is rational?

While it's true that many of the medieval arguments show up in Enlightenment responses to the evidentialist objection, the medieval project of natural theology wasn't an attempt to demonstrate the rationality of religious belief.[5] Medieval philosophers considered belief in God rational *already*, even if it was accepted purely on the say-so of Scripture (that is, by *faith*), rather than by way of arguments. And though natural theology and the Enlightenment project were both part of a long conversation on the topics of faith and reason, the medieval goal was to take something rationally believed by faith and turn it into something rationally believed by reason.[6] Faith is good, the medievals said, but believing by way of reason is better.

Only after Locke was it generally thought that we need arguments for belief in God to be *rational* in the first place. Two events were responsible for the change, both beginning almost simultaneously, and both contributing to the decline of the church's authority. One was the Protestant Reformation, with its ensuing wars of religion.[7] The other was the Scientific Revolution, particularly the conflict between Galileo and the Catholic Church. Both events shook Europe's confidence in the church's claim to timeless truths. Faced with what they saw as a vacuum of authority, many thinkers—now with acute trust issues—felt they could count only on themselves, on their own reason. And this was exactly the position Locke found himself in: he was responding to this loss of universal authority.

CONGENITAL EVIDENTIALISM

Ever since Locke, evidentialism has been the default position in the West. In the century following Locke, the Enlightenment philosopher David Hume, one of philosophy's brilliant bad boys, said that when it comes to religion, "A wise man . . . proportions his belief to the evidence."[8] And in the century after Hume, we find perhaps the most scorching treatise on evidentialism: W. K. Clifford's famous 1877 essay "The Ethics of Belief."[9] Cautioning us of the dire consequences of believing upon insufficient evidence, he wrote,

> If I let myself believe anything on insufficient evidence, there may be no great harm done by the mere belief; it may be true after all, or I may never have occasion to exhibit in outward acts. But I cannot help doing this great wrong towards Man, that I make myself credulous. The danger to society is not merely that it should believe wrong things, though that is great enough; but that it should become credulous, and lose the habit of testing things and inquiring into them; for then it must sink back into savagery. . . . So closely are our duties knit together, that whoso shall keep the whole law, and yet offend in one point he is guilty of all.[10]

Clifford then tied together his stirring exhortation with this famous formula: "it is wrong always, everywhere, and for any one, to believe anything upon insufficient evidence."[11]

The call for evidence seems to be just plain good sense. Yet we get uncomfortable when we read where Clifford approvingly quoted John Milton: "A man may be a heretic in the truth; and if he believe things only because his pastor says so, or the assembly so determine, without knowing other reason, though his belief be true, yet the very truth he holds becomes his heresy."[12] Clifford's point, then, isn't merely that we should accept evidentialism. It's the additional claim that religious beliefs don't meet it.

Closer still to our own day, we find the evidentialist objection taking ever more defiant expressions. In the 1900s Bertrand Russell inspired generations of unbelievers with his Promethean bravado. Alvin Plantinga tells a story about the time someone asked Russell what he would say if he died and found himself facing God and was asked about his persistent disbelief. Russell answered, "I'd say, 'Not enough evidence God! Not enough evidence!'"[13]

Contemporary atheists, then, stand in a long line of evidentialists, a line, ironically, consisting of both believers and unbelievers. So when Sam Harris says that "our credulity must scale with the evidence," we can see the family resemblance: he is just paraphrasing Hume.[14] And yet he's expressing a sentiment that we all find extremely plausible, compelling even. Of course, most believers—despite subscribing to the same evidentialism—won't follow Harris in his charge that belief in God floats "entirely free of reason and evidence."[15]

Evidentialism—the view that all beliefs (including belief in God) must be supported by sufficient evidence—is in our intellectual gene pool. It's one of the few things that believers and unbelievers agree on. It's that rare parcel of common ground.

It's also false.

FOR YOUR ARSENAL

- *Evidentialism*: the view that all beliefs, if they're to be rational, must be supported by sufficient evidence. Nearly all believers have thought that evidentialism is true.

- *The evidentialist objection*: the claim—which is underwritten by evidentialism—that belief in God isn't supported by sufficient evidence and is, therefore, irrational.

- Today's most ardent atheists stand in a long line of unbelievers—from Hume to Russell—who have leveled the evidentialist objection at believers.

2

DOES EVIDENCE NEED EVIDENCE?

Belief in God—like any belief—seems to require evidence. But, since the Enlightenment, atheists have told us that there *is* no such evidence, at least not enough of it. Hitchens, for example, said, "there exists not a shred of respectable evidence" for God's existence.[1] The problem that confronts you, as a believer, then, is this: atheists are demanding evidence for God's existence, and you likely don't have any evidence that would satisfy someone who doesn't already believe in God. This seems like a real problem.

But is it? To answer, we'll first need to know just what evidence is. And then we'll need to look more closely at the claim that rationality requires this evidence. Despite having a lot going for it, evidentialism actually renders all our beliefs irrational. Not what you'd expect.

WHAT IS EVIDENCE?

If I were doubtful about a claim of yours, I might ask *why* you believe such a thing. As David Hume put it, "If I ask why you believe any particular matter of fact, which you relate, you must tell me *some reason*."[2] If, for example, I ask you why you believe that your neighbor Sarah stole your shoes, you might reply, "Look, it was either Sarah or my dog Roscoe, and it certainly wasn't Roscoe—he knows better." You've given me *your* reason for believing that Sarah stole your shoes. You're hoping I'll see that (1) either Sarah stole the shoes or Roscoe stole the shoes, that (2) Roscoe didn't steal the shoes; and that these two assertions provide evidence for your claim that (3) Sarah stole the shoes. In other words, you've given me an *argument*, one with three parts: two premises—statements (1) and (2)—and a conclusion, statement (3). In doing so, you point out two beliefs of yours that evidentially support your belief that Sarah is the culprit. This argument is your evidence.

This kind of evidence might seem different from what we typically think of as evidence. Often we'll think of a weapon that's been dusted for fingerprints—physical evidence. But notice that we always transform physical evidence into an argument. The prosecution presents a gun found in an abandoned car, with the defendant's fingerprints all over it. The intent is to make us form the belief, *A gun with the defendant's fingerprints on it was found in an abandoned car.* And this belief will then feature in an argument of some sort—often complex—that has as its conclusion, *The defendant is guilty.*

In both scenarios, then, we have an argument. We're inferring one belief from other beliefs we hold; we're reasoning from old beliefs to new ones. If we think of an argument as similar to a computer program, with an input and output, we have one or more beliefs as the argument's "input," and another belief as the "output." Old beliefs in, new belief out.

So, if belief in God needs evidence (or "some reason" to believe it, as Hume puts it), it needs a supporting argument, which in turn needs some input beliefs. The question, *Is there evidence or a reason for believing that God exists?* is the same as *Are there any arguments for God's existence?* And if there aren't any arguments—or any good ones—then belief in God is irrational.

At least if evidentialism is true.

CAN WE DO THAT?

Reconsider the Sarah-stole-your-shoes argument. What if I question one of your premises? What if, for example, I ask you why you believe that the only two culprits are Sarah and Roscoe? Presumably, you'll present me with additional beliefs that support *that*. One of the premises in the original argument—*Either Sarah stole the shoes or Roscoe stole the shoes*—would now need to be supported by a new argument. And if I question one of the premises of your new argument, I'm going to ask you to support those new premises. And so on.

Now, for just about every belief each of us holds, someone can ask us why we believe it and expect to receive an argument—a reason—of some sort. But how can we have a reason or argument for every one of our beliefs? For every reason we give, *that* reason will require a reason, which will in turn require yet another reason, and so on, world without end. But of course, we can't have an infinite number of reasons. None of us has that much time on our hands. Or enough patience. All of us have experienced the maddening series of why questions launched at us from the mouths of small children. These why questions, you are quite sure, absolutely must stop. When the great philosopher Ludwig Wittgenstein said, "Explanations come to an end somewhere," he had just visited his niece and nephew.

Let's look at the problem differently. Start with any belief of yours. If evidentialism is true, you should, if you're rational, be able to give some reason for believing it. In other words, you'll have evidence for it, other beliefs supporting the original belief.

These supporting beliefs will also, presumably, have beliefs "beneath" *them*, giving them adequate support. In this way, all our beliefs form a sort of structure or building, with each belief akin to a brick, each brick having at least one brick beneath it (usually more), evidentially supporting it. But, just like in any building, we need a foundation, bricks on which our entire edifice rests.

If evidentialism is true, however, and all beliefs require evidence, then so must your foundational beliefs. But this can't be right, can it? Foundational beliefs have no supporting evidence—they're the foundation. And we've already seen that we need foundational beliefs—we can't have an infinite chain of beliefs supporting beliefs supporting beliefs supporting beliefs . . . Therefore, because you're finite, supporting beliefs (i.e., those used in arguments) must stop at the foundation. Your entire belief structure must be supported by a foundation that itself has no further evidential support. If so, then evidentialism seems to give the wrong answer: it says that foundational beliefs need evidence, and this is a requirement that humans just can't meet.

But does evidentialism really give the wrong answer? Let's hope so. If the beliefs that we all stop at, our foundational beliefs, require evidence in order to be rational, then the beliefs that make up the foundation aren't rational; they don't have the requisite evidential support. They therefore can't provide proper support for the beliefs that they're in charge of supporting. They can't give something they don't have. And here's where we confront the real problem: foundational beliefs are supposed to support our entire belief structure. Yet the whole thing is unsupported and so, according to evidentialism, irrational.

So if evidentialism is true, we have a serious problem—namely, *all* our beliefs are irrational.

A THIRD OPTION

But perhaps there's a way out of this mess. So far we have two options. To see that there's a third, let us change the metaphor from bricks making up a building to links making up a chain. In this metaphor, each link is a belief that is evidentially attached to other beliefs. Given what we've seen so far, our only two options in terms of our new metaphor are an infinite chain of supporting beliefs or else a chain that stops in midair. The third option is this: we could reason in a *circle*, the chain of reasons or beliefs circling back on itself, so that the belief you began with is supported—ultimately—by itself.

This third option looks like a nonstarter, though. Consider the smallest of argument chains, a single link, each end connected to the other (you'll need to bend the link). Suppose you doubt the claim that my truck gets eighty-four miles per gallon. You ask me for a reason to believe such an extraordinary thing. I reply that, well, because my truck gets eighty-four miles per gallon. No doubt you'll be less than impressed, as you should be. I'm attempting to support my claim with itself, pulling it up by its bootstraps.

There are folks, however, who believe that a closed circle of reasons is a fine thing, provided the circle is large enough. Consider a slightly larger circle of beliefs. Suppose I claim, *What the Bible says is true* (which, coincidentally, I *do* believe). Now suppose I support this belief with the following two beliefs: *God is the author of the Bible* and *Whatever God says is true.*[3] To be sure, this is a good reason to believe what the Bible says. But when you ask me why I believe *God is the author of the Bible*, I respond with, *The Bible tells us that God is its author* and, *What the Bible tells us is true.* My belief that what the Bible says is true is supported by my belief that what the Bible says is true. More bootstrapping.

I use this example because many Christians *do* try to reason this way about the Bible. But this is wrong and, as I'll show later, unnecessary. Yet it's not easy to reason people out of this view once they have become so logically promiscuous.

Circularity is tempting because we recognize that we can't keep giving arguments. But what also contributes to its appeal is an implicit belief that evidentialism is true, that every rational belief requires at least one other supporting belief.

So maybe evidentialism is the problem. After all, there are only three options: an infinite chain of reasons, a circular chain, or a chain that comes to an end. The first option is impossible for creatures like us; and if evidentialism is true, the second and third result in irrationality.

But surely—and I think atheists would agree with me here—we're rational in believing many things. Yet if evidentialism is true, neither science nor reason ever leaves the ground.

BASIC BELIEFS—THE FOUNDATION

So evidentialism seems to give us the wrong answer; it tells us that all of us are irrational, all of the time. Can this be true? Suppose you look out your window and see, with delight, the season's first snow. Typically, in such a case you'll believe that it's snowing without running through a quick inference. You won't, for example, turn your attention to the sensations your retinas are receiving and note that these sensations are shaped and colored in ways that make it look like snow is falling, then note that normally your sensory images are reliable, and so probably in this case they *are* reliable and so in all likelihood it really *is* snowing. Rather, you simply find yourself believing that it's snowing.[4]

Similarly for most beliefs formed by our senses, when things appear to us in a certain (hard-to-describe) way, we immediately form beliefs about our environment. And good thing too. Life comes hard and fast. Imagine that you and I are working at a construction site and that, today, I'm in a playful mood. I toss my hammer in your direction, and *then* yell, "Head's up!" But you deftly move out of the way with not a moment to spare, just before pointing your nail gun in my direction. Again, you immediately, to form them without an argument of any sort, found yourself with the belief that, lo, a hammer! And without this ability to form beliefs automatically, to form them without inference, our ancestors would never have had the chance to produce you and me.

Furthermore, ordinary beliefs like, *It's snowing* or, *A hammer!* seem to be perfectly rational. We have a choice then: either evidentialism is true and we're all irrational, or else many of the beliefs we ordinarily accept as rational really *are* rational and evidentialism is false.

The choice seems pretty clear. After all, if evidentialism is true, and *all* beliefs require evidence, then the evidentialist's belief that evidentialism is true is ultimately irrational. Evidentialism itself is ultimately unsupported and therefore self-defeating.

Notice too—and this gets us back to our pressing issue—that any atheist who is also an evidentialist is irrational in believing that belief in God is irrational. After all, her belief that *belief in God is irrational* is itself a belief. Yet because this belief is obviously part of her irrational belief structure, it too is irrational. Denying the legitimacy of foundational beliefs—that is, embracing evidentialism—ends in intellectual suicide.

So at some point, then, we need beliefs that haven't been reasoned *to* at all, beliefs that are not supported by other beliefs by way of arguments. All reasoning needs a place to stand, a foundation. These foundational beliefs (for example, ordinary sense beliefs) are called *basic* beliefs because they're the basis of all our other beliefs. We believe them without any inference whatsoever. And basic beliefs are often perfectly rational.

Rationality, then, can't always require evidence; many rational beliefs are formed automatically with no inference at all.

Evidentialism is quite dead.

FOR YOUR ARSENAL

- *Evidence*: support for a belief in the form of an argument.

- Arguments for our beliefs must ultimately come to an end. There must be beliefs that themselves need no argument to be rational. These foundational beliefs are called *basic beliefs*.

- If evidentialism were true, then all beliefs would be irrational (even the belief in evidentialism) since there would, ultimately, be no rational foundation for our system of beliefs.

3

THEY SHOULD HAVE SEEN THIS COMING

THE "HUMEAN" CONDITION

I t's surprising that evidentialism wasn't pronounced dead long ago. The sheer inadequacy of requiring evidence for every belief is among the Enlightenment's most valuable discoveries. Yet the very people who showed us this inadequacy overlooked it entirely. Love, as you know, is blind.

The Enlightenment philosophers saw that we couldn't argue for the reliability of our cognitive faculties—those various mental faculties that form all our beliefs—even if we wanted to. This is because there often are no arguments. In the last chapter's imaginary inference for your belief about snow, the argument depended essentially on your belief that you can trust your senses. But how do you know that your senses are generally reliable?

The most direct way to support such a belief is to look at your sense perception's track record.[1] Suppose you do this and your research reveals that in most cases, whenever you form a belief based on sense perception, that belief turns out to be true. From this, you can—if you've examined enough cases—reasonably conclude that your senses are generally reliable.

Unfortunately, to check the reliability of your senses, you'll have to use those very senses, assuming all along that they're reliable. But that's the very thing you're trying to convince yourself of, and we've seen that circularity isn't a virtue.

Suppose you're undaunted. Perhaps, you suppose, a less direct approach might do the trick.[2] You point out that your senses work: all these years they've helped you successfully navigate your way through life. Stenger makes this sort of indirect argument: "True, we can't prove our senses are giving us the 'real scoop'. But we have plenty of personal experience that our senses do a good job of alerting us to oncoming cars, warning us when something on the stove has caught fire, and telling us that the baby needs to be fed."[3]

Sadly, this kind of justification also suffers from circularity. Determining that your senses work requires you to use them.[4] You know that the stove is on fire *how*? Right—your senses. And you know that the baby needs food the same way.[5]

We simply don't have noncircular arguments for the reliability of our senses. To put it differently, imagine that Charles has succumbed to an intro philosophy class and he now doubts that his senses are trustworthy. Suppose you try to placate him with the indirect argument, calling his attention to the fact that he's survived this long, and therefore his senses must be reliable. Charles will likely remain unconvinced. He could, he points out, be part of an elaborate psychological experiment: even now, the nefarious scientists are feeding his nerve endings with electrical pulses that produce these exact sensations.

Charles's inability to argue himself out of such doubt is what makes movies like *The Matrix* so compelling. None of us can ever step outside of our senses to compare the visual image behind our eyes with the object "out there." We can't even check to see whether there *is* an "out there" out there, to see whether there's an external world.

David Hume—one of the towering inspirations of contemporary atheism—conceded that we really have no good reason to believe that the world outside of us resembles the perceptual images inside us. Perhaps there isn't an "external" world; it's hard to say. This, he said, is "the whimsical condition of mankind." And the twentieth-century American philosopher Willard Van Orman Quine said that the Humean condition is simply the human condition. Our senses—like us—are destined to remain within the boundary of our skin. Their limitations are ours.

This goes for all the ways we form beliefs, for all our cognitive faculties, whether memory, introspection, or even reason itself. We can never step outside these belief-forming mechanisms to independently verify their reliability.

REASONING ABOUT REASONING

Speaking of reason itself, Hume has a magnificent argument for what he considers, because of his evidentialism, the flimsiness of inferences we might attempt to make about the surrounding world. It's one of the best arguments in all of philosophy.

Hume recognized that we all expect, for example, the sun to rise tomorrow. He then asked what only a philosopher or child could ask: Why do we expect this? The answer is, because the sun has *always* risen. But Hume noticed that this would only count as a good reason if we knew that *the future will resemble the past.* In other words, the argument or reason for believing that the sun will rise tomorrow must be something like this: the sun has always risen in the past, *and because* the future will resemble the past, the sun will rise tomorrow.

But how do we know that the future will be like the past? Because it always has. And it turns out that any argument for our belief that the future will resemble the past will depend on our belief that *the future will resemble the past.* Here's how (this time, instead of reasoning about sunrises, we're reasoning about futures): in the past, the future always resembled the past, and because the future will resemble the past, the future will resemble the past.[6] We would need to first know that the future will resemble the past before we could know that the future will resemble the past. (After thinking such thoughts, Hume was known to clear his head with a game of billiards amongst his friends. My guess is that he was also amongst beer.)

Hume followed his evidentialism where it inevitably led: he concluded that we're irrational in believing that the future will resemble the past. After all, we have no noncircular argument for it; there's no *evidence* to support it. And once this belief goes, so must our belief that the sun will rise tomorrow—and any other belief about things in the world we have yet to see. Inferring future events from past events[7]—called *induction*—is how we gain precious experience, that mother of all teachers. And it's irrational. Try not to think about that the next time you cross a busy street. (Undoubtedly, you won't give it a thought.)

By the way, could those cars—those that experience has convinced you to avoid—cause your death upon impact? Well, that, too, is difficult to say, if Hume is to be believed. Hume pointed out that we never actually *see* one event cause another. We really can't say, for example, that the cue ball itself (Hume didn't know about cars) *causes* the eight ball to move toward the corner pocket. We only ever see the pool balls' actual motions, but never the underlying causal connection. And Hume is right: we never see a mysterious hidden cause. After all, it's logically possible that an invisible fairy moves the eight ball, taking the occasion of the close proximity of the two balls to move the second toward the corner pocket.

But of course, Hume acknowledged, we could never actually believe such a far-fetched story. Despite his doubts about the external world, induction, and fundamental causation, Hume noted with relief that "Nature will always maintain her rights, and prevail in the end over any abstract reasoning whatsoever."[8] In other words, we can't help but believe that the future will resemble the past or that the sun will rise tomorrow or that the cue ball causes the eight ball to move. Our instincts are just too strong for philosophy to overcome. We're irrational, but it keeps us alive. A world of whimsy.

Thomas Reid, a contemporary of Hume and a fellow Scot, watched with amusement as Hume despaired over our inability to justify our cognitive faculties. Reid was well known during his lifetime but his works quickly went dormant, to be only recently rediscovered by philosophers like Plantinga and Wolterstorff. Reid was the one genuine bright spot in Enlightenment philosophy; he kept his wits about him. Here he directed his (un)common sense at Hume (the "sceptic"):

> The sceptic asks me, Why do you believe the existence of the external object which you perceive? This belief, sir, is none of my manufacture; it came from the mint of Nature; it bears her image and superscription; and, if it is not right, the fault is not mine; I ever took it upon trust, and without suspicion. Reason, says the sceptic, is the only judge of truth, and you ought to throw off every opinion and every belief that is not grounded on reason. Why, sir, should I believe the faculty of reason more than that of perception? They came both out of the same shop, and were made by the same artist; and if he puts one piece of false ware into my hands, what should hinder him from putting another?[9]

Reid was pointing out that Hume used reason the entire time he was reasoning about (and doubting) cognitive faculties like sense perception. But why trust reason, asks Reid? Why not require a justification for that too? The answer, of course, is that Hume's entire critical project would have thereby collapsed. To question reason is to trust it.

Reid's point is that favoring reason over our senses (as Hume implicitly did) amounts to arbitrary preferential treatment. And Reid sees Hume's failure to question reason, not as loyalty to reason, but as a failure of nerve. But I think Hume may simply have had a blind spot. Love can cause a man to overlook many things others won't.

EXPERIENCE THE INPUT

We can't give an argument for the reliability of our cognitive (i.e., belief-forming) faculties without trusting them first. Whether it be our senses, our reason, or our memory, we must trust them in order to use them, and use them to argue for them. Again, evidentialism—the requirement that all rational beliefs be evidentially supported by arguments—gives us the wrong answer.

This doesn't mean, however, that once we rid ourselves of evidentialism, *anything* goes. It's not as if your belief that it's snowing outside is capricious or random. Even if it isn't supported by an argument, it still rests on something. *Something* causes it. But what?

In the case of the season's first snow, you look out the window and your eyes are stimulated by light waves, which your brain interprets as shapes and colors, and then interprets as a snowy scene. The world appears to you in that familiar snowy way and you automatically find yourself with the belief that it's snowing.

A visual *experience* causes your belief; it's not inferred from other beliefs. Similarly for smells and sounds, tastes and touches. The sensation of pain in your lower back immediately causes you to believe that you're in pain—with no effort or inference on your part. The experience automatically "triggers" the belief.

This experience—what it feels like from the inside—is often very difficult to describe. Take, for example, my memory belief that I had coffee this morning. The internal memory experience associated with this belief isn't really a mental *image*, but something else, something vague and inchoate, but distinct enough to cause my coffee belief. It feels memoryish. To describe it any more is surprisingly difficult. In fact, even straightforward visual experiences are hard to describe. How does the snow outside appear to me—what does it look like? Well, white . . . snowy . . . you know, that common snow-like appearance.

My point here is that we don't ordinarily *infer* beliefs like these; they're caused by experiences and not by reasoning from other beliefs. And our perceptual beliefs are usually entirely rational because they're based on the right kinds of experience.

But what are the right kinds of experiences? That will depend on the particular cognitive faculty, and on whether the faculty is operating properly, and whether it's operating in the proper environment. For example, your vision may not function as it ought if you're trying to spot a sea lion a quarter mile away in the ocean at dusk. Your eyes simply aren't meant to see objects of that size at that distance and in that light. But if the sea lion is ten feet away from where you're standing on the jetty, and in broad daylight (with no glare), then you would likely be rational in believing there's a sea lion.

Something similar applies to our reasoning faculty when we infer new beliefs from old ones. This faculty, too, must be functioning properly and in the appropriate environment. My ability to follow arguments will be diminished if I'm under great duress, say, while being mugged or falling from a roof.

WHAT MAKES A BELIEF RATIONAL?

Because evidentialism is wrong, beliefs can be rational even without evidence. But what exactly makes a belief rational? Sometimes it *is* evidence (an argument); sometimes it's experience.[10] In either case, we now have enough to characterize rationality more precisely:

> *A rational belief is one formed by a properly functioning cognitive faculty operating in the appropriate environment.*[11]

We should add that the goal of these cognitive faculties must be to get at the truth. The goal of some cognitive faculties may not be to produce true beliefs, but beliefs that—although not true—provide some other benefit, such as survival. For example, suppose your doctor informs you that you have a serious form of cancer that, in all likelihood, will kill you (he doesn't put it quite that way). Because of your cheery disposition and rosy outlook, you nevertheless believe that your chances are much better than the facts warrant. And suppose your optimism does help you survive the disease. In such a case, you still wouldn't have been rational in believing that you would survive the cancer, even though there may be a cognitive faculty that is meant to override your normal reasoning powers when in certain kinds of danger.

But even though we have decent definitions of "evidence" and "rational belief," it still may be that belief in God comes nowhere near being rational in this more accurate sense. We'll have to address this, but we can say, at least, that Enlightenment-style evidentialism suffers from a fairly significant defect: it's simply not true.

So the Enlightenment left us with an untenable intellectual heritage. If we were to require arguments to support any belief whatsoever, then our entire belief system would be rendered irrational. The rationalist's standard is, ironically, unreasonable. Without assistance, reason collapses under its own weight. Our cognitive faculties are a team.

FOR YOUR ARSENAL

- There are no noncircular arguments for the reliability of any of our cognitive (belief-forming) faculties.

- Beliefs formed by our cognitive faculties—which are usually the beliefs we're most confident of—must be assumed rather than inferred. That is, they're basic beliefs.

- Even though basic beliefs have no supporting arguments, they're not formed arbitrarily. Rather, they're immediately caused or triggered by *experiences*.

- *Rational belief*: a belief formed by a properly functioning cognitive faculty operating in the appropriate environment.

4

TRUST ME

YES, BUT . . .

F air enough, the atheist might reply. Even if we grant that evidentialism is false and concede that we don't—indeed cannot—have arguments for all of our beliefs, there's still a vast difference between science, say, and belief in God. Science earns its knowledge through honest toil, whereas religious beliefs are gotten on the cheap—by a mere blind leap. Faith is too easy, according to Christopher Hitchens, too facile:

> If one must have faith in order to believe something, or believe
> *in* something, then the likelihood of that something having any
> truth or value is considerably diminished. The harder work of
> inquiry, proof, and demonstration is infinitely more rewarding,
> and has confronted us with findings far more "miraculous" and
> "transcendent" than any theology.[1]

And even if it turned out that what we believe by faith was true, whatever pleasure we gained from that fact would be a stolen one.

This supposes, of course, that Hitchens knew what faith is and how it differs from science. The difference between science and faith is fairly clear from his comment. When he used the terms "proof," and "demonstration," he meant—if he meant anything specific—argument or inference. Believing by way of an argument is considerably more reliable than believing without one.

Naturally, that's entirely wrong. It's old news (to you now) that many of our most important and most reliable beliefs are held on the basis of experience, not by way of "proofs" or "demonstrations." Like everyone else, scientists need noninferential basic beliefs. So, lack of evidential support (i.e., the presence of basic beliefs) isn't the difference between faith and science.

What *is* the difference then? And more pressing, what exactly is faith?

BELIEVING WHAT YOU KNOW AIN'T SO

These are important questions. Even the early church fathers were keenly interested in the nature of faith, and particularly the relation between faith and reason. Within a century or so after the apostolic teachings were set down in Scripture, Tertullian asked, "What indeed has Athens to do with Jerusalem?" He meant, in other words, what has Greek philosophy (i.e., reason) to do with the Christian faith?[2] Our questions, therefore, are part of a long and respectable legacy. Unfortunately the terms "faith" and "reason" are, as philosophers like to say, multiply ambiguous.

Hitchens and other atheists would doubtless agree with Archie Bunker: "Faith is something that you believe that nobody in his right mind would believe."[3] Or maybe they think, as Mark Twain did, that faith is "believing what you know ain't so." But, not surprisingly, we find a slightly different view of faith when we look at Scripture.

Take, for example, the Bible's portrayal of Abraham. The substance of Abraham's faith was that he simply believed what God told him, despite the apparent improbabilities (Romans 4; Hebrews 11:8–11). Biblical faith is taking God at his word, trusting what he says. Faith is believing God's *testimony*.[4]

And this is the sense of "faith" that John Locke used in the original context of evidentialism. For Locke, faith is "the assent to any proposition, not thus made out by the deductions of reason, but upon the credit of the proposer, as coming from God in some extraordinary way of communicating."[5] Faith, again, is believing something on the say-so of God himself, rather than by way of an argument (i.e., rather than "by the deductions of reason"). Although I might be able to impressively argue that Jesus is the Son of God, if I believed this doctrine only by way of my arguments, I wouldn't be simply taking God at his word. I wouldn't believe by way of faith, but, rather, by way of reason.

We use the term "faith" similarly in other contexts. Suppose my son tells me that he saw a three-legged dog on our block. I don't need evidence. I trust that what he says is true. I have faith in him. I believe his testimony. When I use a map to find the Oregon coast, I trust the map; I follow the map on faith. Similarly I believe what my physics textbook tells me about the existence of electrons. I've never actually seen an electron (nor has anyone else), but I take it on faith that the author is telling the truth.

In all these cases, I believe by way of testimony and therefore by way of faith. We can now define "faith" as follows:

Faith is believing something by way of testimony.

Of course, this includes believing something by way of *God's* testimony or say-so, but it includes far more than that. Anytime I believe something on the say-so of someone or something else (a map or book), I believe by way of faith.

Notice then, that *faith* refers to a way, method, or process of believing (i.e., by way of testimony). But the word *faith* can also be used in other ways, ways we'll want to keep separate to avoid confusion.

Sometimes, when we say we believe something by faith, we mean that we learned some bit of information from Scripture. *Faith*, in this sense, means "the Bible." Faith teaches, for example, that fire didn't consume the burning bush, and science teaches that fire is luminous gases produced by a chemical reaction. Science is one source, the Bible another.[6] This "source" version of *faith* is fine, but not relevant for our discussion. Better to use "the Bible" whenever we mean the source of information. Notice, however, when we take the Bible at its word, we're believing by faith in *our* sense. To be sure, the source of testimony is Scripture, but our use of "faith" is pointing out something about us, not the source.

Another common use of "faith" means "belief in God," as in "faith versus unbelief." Faith here is contrasted with the absence of belief in God. This, too, is a fine way to use the term. But when we want to refer to belief in God, we will just use "belief in God." The extra effort is more than worth it.

One thing more before we move on. We've defined faith, but what exactly is reason? We've implicitly assumed an answer throughout, but now is the time to make it explicit. Recall Locke's view that faith is not the result of "the deductions of reason." Reason is that faculty which performs "deductions" or, in general, inferences.[7] It's the cognitive faculty that we use to *give an argument*.[8]

TAKING THEIR WORD FOR IT

Because faith is believing by way of testimony, let's look at how pervasive testimony is in our lives. You know your name, where you live, your age, that your parents are indeed your parents, all by way of testimony. I know that I live in Moscow, Idaho, because maps and signs have told me so. I have never directly *seen* (or smelled or tasted) that this state is Idaho, or that this country is the United States.[9]

Nor have I inferred these things by way of an argument.

With respect to my belief that I live in Idaho, I *could* formulate a coherent story into which a whole host of beliefs fit together, thereby reasoning that the best explanation for this coherent story is that I really do live in Idaho.[10] But I don't make this sort of effort; I've usually got better things to do, as do most of us.

So, believing something by way of testimony is often an excellent thing. In fact, you and I are alive to consider the virtues of testimony because of our reliance on it. Recall that the Enlightenment's one ray of light was Thomas Reid. Reid recognized the centrality of testimony centuries ago, while Hume was still puzzling over our whimsical condition. Said Reid,

> The wise author of nature hath planted in the human mind a propensity to rely upon human testimony before we can give a reason for doing so. This indeed puts our judgment almost entirely in the power of those who are about us in the first period of life; but this is necessary both to our preservation and to our improvement. If children were so framed as to pay no regard to testimony or authority, they must, in the literal sense, perish for lack of knowledge.[11]

Reid referred to our propensity to believe testimony as "credulity." Today, we use the term differently, meaning something like "gullibility." But for Reid it was simply our natural willingness to believe what others tell us.

Credulity is a type of belief-forming mechanism, like sense perception, reason, and memory, so we can add it to our list of cognitive faculties. And, using our definition of rationality, we are rational in believing testimony insofar as our credulity mechanism is functioning properly in the appropriate environment.

Although we don't form our testimonial beliefs by way of an argument—by way of an inference—it isn't as if such beliefs are based on nothing whatsoever. Rather, they're based on a type of experience, a complex input from our senses (hearing a person or seeing the words on a page) such that we just find ourselves believing the testimony. In these cases, our sense experience does double duty. It first triggers a belief *that* there's a testifier and *that* the testimony is such and such. It then triggers belief *in* the content of the testimony.

Obviously, not all environments are amenable to our credulity mechanism. Although our credulity knows no bounds while we're very young, we learn to fine-tune it as we discover which sorts of people are reliable (or not) about certain topics. Plantinga says, "I believe you when you tell me about your summer vacation, but not when you tout on television the marvelous virtues of the deodorant you have been hired to sell."[12] Charlatans, liars, and lion-maned tel-evangelists have their use. They help us refine our cognitive faculties.

Not to put too fine a point on it, testimony is important. In fact, testimony "makes possible intellectual achievement and culture; testi-mony is the very foundation of civilization."[13] Our knowledge would be scanty indeed if we couldn't learn from other people's experience, if we couldn't trust the testimony of books, teachers, and parents.

And yet testimony is even more important than that. Not merely must we depend on testimony when learning from other people's experience; our own experiences, like those associated with sense per-ception and memory, are also based on testimony. This is another of the Enlightenment's rejected lessons.

GROW UP!

The Enlightenment was only partially aware of testimony's role in our intellectual lives; and the part it recognized, it disdained as childish and immature. After all, what could be more childlike than believing your parents and teachers?

But, said most Enlightenment philosophers, we're behaving just as childishly when we listen to pastors, priests, and the Bible. And so the Enlightenment's main spokesman, German philosopher Immanuel Kant, defined "enlightenment" as a type of growing up, or coming of age: "Enlightenment is man's release from his self-incurred tutelage." He explained,

Immaturity is the inability to use one's understanding without guidance from another. This immaturity is self-imposed when its cause lies not in lack of understanding, but in lack of resolve and courage to use it without guidance from another. *Sapere Aude!* [Dare to Know!] "Have courage to use your own understanding!"—that is the motto of enlightenment.[14]

Hume had awakened Kant from his "dogmatic slumbers," alerting him to mankind's whimsical condition.[15] Yet Kant respected Newton's new science above all things, even above Hume. And because Hume's skepticism about causation, induction, and the external world undermined Newtonian physics, Kant set out to overturn Hume's pessimistic conclusions.

But Kant's solution ends up being a type of *über*-skepticism—doubt run amok—leaving Hume's version looking much kinder and gentler. Kant had quickly encountered the same barrier Hume had: there is simply no way to argue that the visual images behind our eyes match the world "out there." In fact, Kant concluded, we can't know anything about a world outside our minds, other than perhaps that there is one (and he based this measly conclusion on tissue-thin arguments).

And yet Kant never admitted that he had simply strengthened Humean skepticism. Instead, he claimed that, because causation and induction apply to only the images of sense perception behind our eyes, we need not be skeptical about causation and induction. We have, after all, special and immediate access to these images. We no longer need wonder whether our visual images match some objective external world, or whether induction and causation apply to objects outside our minds. All we really care about, Kant triumphantly claimed, is the world of ideas within our skulls. That's all we can know anyway. There's no longer a question of whether our senses are reliable, of whether our ideas accurately match the world.

But only because Kant lowered the bar. It's much easier to make the standards fit your philosophy than vice versa.

Now, for all Kant's heroic talk of using his own understanding, his refusal to acknowledge the Enlightenment's disappointing results seems less than valiant. To echo Reid, it seems a failure of nerve as much as a failure of reason.

Despite reason's inability to single-handedly support our commonsense beliefs, the French revolutionaries still went right ahead and replaced Christian churches with temples to Reason. They built guillotines too.[16] Reason is like most tools: helpful if used properly, dangerous if abused.

FAITH IS EVERYWHERE

Again, as Reid pointed out, to know anything about the world we must accept what our senses tell us. We can "dare to know" only if we trust the "testimony of our senses" (as Hume called it).[17] Similarly for reason, memory, and our other cognitive faculties. We simply have to take our faculties at their word.

And by taking reason and sense perception at their word, we trust their testimony. Testimony, therefore, is foundational to everything we believe. Without trusting our cognitive faculties, we could never believe anything.

Moreover, remember, believing something on the basis of testimony is faith. Therefore, faith is the starting point for all we know and believe. Anselm of Canterbury had a much more reasonable motto than the Enlightenment's, one that hints at the importance of faith: "*Credo ut intelligam*," that is, "I believe that I may understand." Reid put it a bit differently, saying that the unjust must live by faith no less than the just.[18]

So, when Stenger complains that science and reason don't rely on faith, he's missed the Enlightenment's important (and unintended) lessons about faith, reason, and evidence. "The theist argument that science and reason are also based on faith is specious," he says. "Faith is belief in the absence of supportive evidence. Science is belief in the presence of supportive evidence. And reason is just the procedure by which humans ensure that their conclusions are consistent with the theory that produced them and with the data that test these conclusions."[19] Stenger is right about one thing: having faith *is* believing something without having an argument for it ("belief in the absence of supportive evidence"). But Stenger's failure to realize that science, too, is based on faith (because everything we believe is, ultimately) is a massive mistake. Yet it's as common as it is colossal.

QUESTION AUTHORITY? SAYS WHO?

Notice, too, that when we accept someone's testimony—or some*thing's* testimony (e.g., a map or our memory)—we're taking that testimony on the authority of the testifier. We aren't, that is, relying on our "own understanding" but instead are depending on someone or something other than ourselves. But in delightful irony, the Enlightenment's main goal was to reject tradition and authority.

Moreover, today's atheists are bewildered when they find believers who won't accept every jot and tittle of contemporary science. But as a friend of mine rightly said, "Don't tell me to question authority and then get upset when I question your authority."[20]

In any case, atheists can't reasonably criticize belief in God simply because it depends on faith. Perhaps there is some other problem with it; but the problem isn't faith *per se*. Everyone needs a little faith. More than a little, in fact.

FOR YOUR ARSENAL

- *Faith*: believing something by way of testimony.

- Faith is more widespread than we realize. It is necessary, for example, for knowing your name, knowing that your parents really are your parents, and learning from a map or book.

- Faith is required for believing the "testimony of the senses," as well as the beliefs delivered to us by our other cognitive faculties.

- Because all our beliefs are formed by our cognitive faculties, all our beliefs ultimately depend on faith.

5

DARWIN'S DOUBT

HUME HAD A POINT

F aith—in the general sense of believing something by way of testimony—is the foundation of everything we believe. But does that mean we must trust *all* testimony? Surely not. Although Abraham trusted God, he wouldn't have believed *just anybody* who told him things that God told him. As we mature, we become more adept at deciding whose testimony to accept or reject.

Now, couldn't we charitably interpret the Enlightenment's message as merely the reasonable plea that we rein in our credulity? Perhaps.

But why think that our credulity isn't already functioning perfectly well? The real question for us at this point, then, is who—and what—should we put our faith in? What if we're already trusting the right sources? For the next two chapters, we'll look more closely at the trust we put in our cognitive faculties. Maybe we should be more circumspect than we ordinarily are.

After all, there's something to be said for Hume's skepticism; it's not as if he had *no* point. He asked some of the best questions about our cognitive faculties that anyone has asked. Hume's answers left something to be desired, yet to his credit, he sometimes saw where his skepticism led:

> Where am I, or what? From what causes do I derive my existence, and to what condition shall I return? Whose favour shall I court, and whose anger must I dread? What beings surround me? and on whom have I any influence, or who have any influence on me? I am confounded with all these questions, and begin to fancy myself in the most deplorable condition imaginable, inviron'd with the deepest darkness, and utterly depriv'd of the use of every member and faculty.[1]

WHO KNOWS? NOT AGNOSTICS.

And, unlike us, Hume (we'll see) had good reason to doubt his faculties. Reid's question is important enough to repeat: "Why, sir, should I believe the faculty of reason more than that of perception?" After all, "They came both out of the same shop, and were made by the same artist; and if he puts one piece of false ware into my hands, what should hinder him from putting another?"[2] Here is the crucial question: Where did our cognitive faculties come from?

Of course, this is just a version of the question, where did *we* come from? It's a question of ultimate origins, of *how humans got here.* And Hume didn't know how we got here; nor did he know where the universe came from or whether God exists. He thought we simply don't have enough to go on: "A total suspense of judgment," he said, "is here our only reasonable resource."[3]

Plantinga points out that Hume's *agnosticism* (i.e., Hume's confession of ignorance) about our origins implies agnosticism about the origins of our cognitive faculties. Plantinga then employs Hume's agnosticism about our cognitive faculties to show that, for Hume, unbelief is irrational. Look at it this way. Hume doesn't know where these faculties came from; they could have formed entirely by accident or have been designed by a malevolent demon for all Hume knows. There's no reason, therefore, for Hume to think that our faculties will provide more true beliefs than false ones. That is, if Hume suspends judgment about the origins and purpose of our cognitive faculties, then there's no telling (for him) whether our faculties are reliable—whether they generally provide us with *true* beliefs. Of course, in the everyday business of life, we *assume* they're reliable, but—in our quiet contemplative moments—just how probable *is* this assumption?[4]

The answer for Hume, according to Plantinga, is "Who knows?" That would, after all, depend on how our cognitive faculties got here. And Hume declares ignorance on that point. On the one hand, it may be highly likely that our cognitive faculties are reliable, that they tend to produce true beliefs in us. On the other hand, the probability may be very low. It's difficult or impossible to say. In other words, Plantinga explains, the reasonable position for Hume to take with respect to the reliability of his faculties is agnosticism. Hume should simply withhold judgment about their reliability.[5]

But this, continues Plantinga, leads to further problems. Serious ones. Any belief of Hume's will obviously be produced by his belief-forming cognitive faculties (what else?). That means that Hume has a reason to withhold judgment about the truth of each and every belief: all were produced by faculties that came from who-knows-where. But of course his belief that he should withhold judgment on everything is itself a belief. Hume should then withhold judgment about whether he should withhold judgment. And so he *shouldn't* believe that he should withhold judgment (nor should he believe that he should with-hold judgment).[6] He's going to feel *that* in the morning.

And he can't escape his predicament by simply assuming that his senses are reliable. That's because he's questioning his faculties. Moreover, that belief (that his belief-forming faculties are reliable) would come from those very faculties.[7] As Reid said, "If a man's honesty were called into question, it would be ridiculous to refer it to the man's own word, whether he be honest or not."[8] Mistrust always feeds on itself—and its destruction is widespread. Ask anyone who has been lied to.

ATHEISM: NOW YOU KNOW IT, NOW YOU DON'T

But Plantinga isn't finished. There's another kind of unbelief—a stronger kind. Hume was *agnostic* about whether God exists and therefore about whether humans were designed or merely a cosmic accident. It wasn't that Hume believed that God *doesn't* exist; rather, he didn't form *any opinion*—he didn't know *what* to think. He neither believed that God existed, nor that God didn't exist.

But there's another option—atheism. To be sure, neither atheists nor agnostics believe in God, but atheists have the further belief that God *doesn't* exist, whereas agnostics would refrain from taking such a stand.[9]

Hume had no story about our origins; neither did his atheist contemporaries. But today's atheists do. They firmly believe that their cognitive faculties are the result of blind, unguided evolution. Richard Dawkins says—with an audible sigh—that Darwin finally made it possible for atheists to be intellectually fulfilled.[10] At long last, science has provided unbelievers with a story of human origins. No more of Hume's wandering in a dark labyrinth.

Because today's atheists have a story of our origins, they also have a story of the origins and purpose of our cognitive faculties. Our cognitive faculties are reliable because evolution—that "blind watchmaker," as Dawkins calls it—fashions these faculties for our survival. And to survive (which we're doing, it must be admitted), our cognitive faculties must accurately hook up with the world, giving us true beliefs more often than not. It absolutely would not do to believe that there's not a saber-toothed tiger in front of me when there is. Those organisms that survive have been given a gift, albeit a gift given by no one at all.

But evolution doesn't necessarily sift for cognitive mechanisms that produce true beliefs. At least not directly. The philosopher of science Ronald Giere puts it this way:

> For early humans . . . [their] problems were the very specific ones of doing the right things enough of the time. Thus, human physical and cognitive abilities evolved together to promote appropriate actions, not to promote the discovery of anything like general truths about the world. In fact, these two goals are often in conflict. For example, given that one has to act quickly and thus on the basis of only partial information, it is usually better for long-run survival to overestimate the presence of predators and take evasive action even when it is not really necessary.[11]

We're of course familiar with this sort of neurotic behavior in animals. (It's why we never get a chance to pet wild bunnies.) But Giere goes on to the real question: "How did creatures with the evolved physical and cognitive capabilities of contemporary humans come to create the vast body of scientific knowledge that now exists, including evolutionary theory itself?"[12]

All evolution cares about is survival, getting the organism in the right places at the right times so that it can reproduce. And of course, organisms don't need beliefs to do *that*. Viruses and antibodies war with one another without so much as second (or first) thought. And each has its share of victories; each is remarkably successful at identifying threats, locating sources of fuel, and otherwise navigating through a world bent on killing them. They perform fantastic feats of staying alive without any beliefs at all, much less true ones. And this is probably so for even more complex organisms. In fact, it isn't clear at what point organisms begin having beliefs. Do dogs? Maybe. Cats? Surely not. Cockroaches? Unlikely. Yet all have a talent for survival.

Even Darwin had some misgivings about the reliability of *human* beliefs. He wrote, "With me the horrid doubt always arises whether the convictions of man's mind, which has been developed from the mind of lower animals, are of any value or at all trustworthy. Would any one trust in the convictions of a monkey's mind, if there are any convictions in such a mind?"[13]

Given unguided evolution, "Darwin's Doubt" is a reasonable one. Even given unguided or blind evolution, it's difficult to say how probable it is that creatures—even creatures like us—would ever develop true beliefs. In other words, given the blindness of evolution, and that its ultimate "goal" is merely the survival of the organism (or simply the propagation of its genetic code), a good case can be made that atheists find themselves in a situation very similar to Hume's.

The Nobel Laureate and physicist Eugene Wigner echoed this sentiment: "Certainly it is hard to believe that our reasoning power was brought, by Darwin's process of natural selection, to the perfection which it seems to possess."[14] That is, atheists have a reason to doubt whether evolution would result in cognitive faculties that produce mostly true beliefs. And if so, then they have reason to withhold judgment on the reliability of their cognitive faculties. Like before, as in the case of Humean agnostics, this ignorance would, if atheists are consistent, spread to all of their other beliefs, including atheism and evolution.[15] That is, because there's no telling whether unguided evolution would fashion our cognitive faculties to produce mostly true beliefs, atheists who believe the standard evolutionary story must reserve judgment about whether any of their beliefs produced by these faculties are true. This includes the belief in the evolutionary story. Believing in unguided evolution comes built in with its very own reason not to believe it.

This will be an unwelcome surprise for atheists. To make things worse, this news comes after the heady intellectual satisfaction that Dawkins claims evolution provided for thoughtful unbelievers. The very story that promised to save atheists from Hume's agnostic predicament has the same depressing ending.

WHAT IF SURVIVAL *DID*
REQUIRE TRUE BELIEFS?

It's obviously difficult for us to imagine what the world would be like in such a case where we have the beliefs that we do and yet very few of them are true. This is, in part, because we strongly believe that our beliefs *are* true (presumably not all of them are, since to err is human—if we knew which of our beliefs were false, they would no longer be our beliefs).

Suppose you're not convinced that we could survive without reliable belief-forming capabilities, without mostly true beliefs. Then, according to Plantinga, you have all the fixins for a nice argument in favor of God's existence.[16] For perhaps you also think that—given evolution plus atheism—the probability is pretty low that we'd have faculties that produced mostly true beliefs. In other words, your view isn't "who knows?" On the contrary, you think it's unlikely that blind evolution has the skill set for manufacturing reliable cognitive mechanisms. And perhaps, like most of us, you think that we actually have reliable cognitive faculties and so actually have mostly true beliefs. If so, then you would be reasonable to conclude that atheism is pretty unlikely. Your argument, then, would go something like this: if atheism is true, then it's unlikely that most of our beliefs are true; but most of our beliefs *are* true, therefore atheism is probably false.

Notice something else. The atheist naturally thinks that our belief in God is false. That's just what atheists *do*. Nevertheless, most human beings have believed in a god of some sort, or at least in a supernatural realm. But suppose, for argument's sake, that this widespread belief really *is* false, and that it merely provides survival benefits for humans, a coping mechanism of sorts. If so, then we would have additional evidence—on the atheist's own terms—that evolution is more interested in useful beliefs than in true ones. Or, alternatively, if evolution really is concerned with true beliefs, then maybe the widespread belief in God would be a kind of "evolutionary" evidence for his existence.

You've got to wonder.

SHOOTING YOURSELF IN THE FOOT
(OR SOMEWHERE WORSE)

Notice that the intellectual defect of both agnosticism and atheism isn't that they can't produce an argument for the reliability of reason, sense perception, introspection, memory, and the like. No one can do that. That is, no one can avoid circularity while at the same time attempting to argue for the reliability of these mechanisms.

Rather, the problem is that on each of these views—on agnosticism and atheism—there's reason to believe something (namely, that we should withhold judgment about the truth of each and every belief) that paradoxically undermines *all* beliefs, even belief in agnosticism and atheism. Both views are, in other words, *self-defeating*—forms of intellectual suicide. If this is genuinely the case, neither position is a good bet.

Believers, on the other hand, have a coherent story of our cognitive faculties' origins—or at least a story that doesn't undermine those same faculties. According to Christianity, God designed our faculties, just as he designed the world in which these faculties guide us. Compatibility is built in; the manufacturer intended a reliable cognitive fit between humans and the world.

But again, the Christian's story isn't an argument for the reliability of our senses or reason or memory—after all, we come to believe the story through those very same cognitive faculties. Rather, the point (for this chapter) is that Christianity doesn't suffer from the self-defeat that afflicts agnosticism and atheism.

WE'RE GETTING CLOSER

We've seen that evidentialists are wrong to demand arguments for *all* our beliefs. Many of our beliefs—those we called "basic" beliefs—are automatically triggered by our cognitive faculties by the input of experience. And we saw that trusting our cognitive faculties is akin to trusting the testimony of other people: we simply take our faculties at their word, unless we have good reason to question them. Every one of our beliefs, therefore, ultimately rests on faith. We then saw that atheists have good reason to question their cognitive faculties, and this puts them in an unenviable position: their doubt must be doubted, which in turn, must also be doubted, which in turn . . . well, as you can see, atheism seems untenable on its own terms.

But we're still left with the question, *Is it rational to believe in God?* Perhaps the Christian *can* make sense of the reliability of sense perception and reason by appealing to a divine designer—but they can only do so, it seems, if it's rational to believe that a designer exists. Remember, to be rational, a belief must be formed by a properly functioning cognitive faculty operating in the appropriate environment. But is belief in God formed by such a faculty? Can belief in God be basic?

If not, then it seems that the evidentialist is right after all, at least about belief in God: it had better be supported by evidence—by *arguments.*

The problem is, only a small fraction of Christians have come to believe in God through an argument. Very few have carefully considered arguments for and against God's existence, or investigated the reliability of Scripture, or the fulfillment of Old Testament prophesies, or the coherence of doctrines like the Trinity and incarnation. Fewer still have believed on the basis of such considerations.

When Christians believe in God without argument, then, it had better be in the *basic* way. But basic beliefs—at least rational ones—are caused by some sort of experience working through some properly functioning faculty (and in an appropriate environment). Is there any such thing for belief in God?

Why, yes, which is why, as we'll see, belief in God can be entirely rational without being based on any argument whatsoever—the exact situation in which nearly all believers find themselves. Knowing how belief in God can be rational *and* basic will allow Christians to better understand the nature of their faith, thereby strengthening it. And it would be difficult to overstate the importance of the calm confidence that comes with this lesson.

FOR YOUR ARSENAL

- *Agnostics*: unbelievers who, while not believing in God, refrain from saying that God doesn't exist. *Atheists*: unbelievers who believe that God doesn't exist.

- Agnostics like Hume (who didn't have the theory of evolution) don't know what to believe about our cognitive faculties' origins. They therefore have to suspend judgment about whether these faculties are reliable. But since the agnostics' belief that they must suspend judgment is also a belief, they must suspend judgment about agnosticism itself (as well as all their other beliefs). Agnosticism becomes self-defeating.

- As even Darwin suggested, atheists who believe in unguided evolution have a powerful reason not to trust their cognitive faculties, since such faculties did not necessarily evolve to form true beliefs but merely beliefs conducive to survival. Such atheists thereby find themselves in a self-defeating situation similar to that of Humean agnostics.

6

TAKING GOD FOR GRANTED

A PROBLEM

Even if rationality requires faith, faith needs discrimination. Some basic beliefs are only so much intellectual riffraff. To be sure, many beliefs have impeccable credentials, but I don't want to fraternize with beliefs created by malfunctioning cognitive faculties, or by faculties operating in subpar conditions. Unlike an owl's eyes, mine won't work in near-total darkness. Maybe that *is* Bigfoot there; but it may also be the faint shadow of a tree, so very hard to discern against the night. Similarly, my ears don't operate as they ought in a vacuum, and testimony leads me astray when the testifier is an accomplished liar or is herself deceived.

And doesn't this last type of situation characterize belief in God? Haven't believers been sold a bill of goods, intentionally or not? To be sure, we form our ordinary, *uncontroversial* basic beliefs—those fashioned by our senses, reason, or memory—using mechanisms that every standard human comes equipped with. But—and here's the real issue—there's *no* such mechanism for belief in God. Without inference or arguments (and *good* ones at that), Christian faith is a leap in the dark, a Kierkegaardian belief in the face of the absurd.[1] And even if belief in God *were* produced by a standard faculty, it would probably be just the credulity mechanism run amok.

These are good points.

Well, how *do* Christians typically come to believe in God and in the "great things of the gospel" (as Jonathan Edwards put it)?[2] As we said, we don't usually believe by way of arguments, which is why belief in God is characterized as a "leap" or "believing what you know ain't so." Although some Christians (C. S. Lewis comes to mind) might come to believe through arguments, most of us don't. Of course, we might be able to *give* an argument if we're asked for one, but that's entirely different from believing *on the basis* of one. The argument is something we construct after, even because, we believe.

The question "Why do you believe in God?" can be taken in a number of ways. On its face, it just means, "On what do you base *your* belief in God?" And often the person asks in order to judge whether your reasons for believing are good ones. But other times the questioner may want you to convince *him*: "Why should *I* believe in God?" Each version of the question will probably have its own answer(s). To confuse the two is to court trouble.

For now, we'll focus on the first and obvious sense, "Why do *you* believe in God?" I want to suggest that there are many times when believers can rationally answer, "Why wouldn't I?"

Yet this response seems—how can I put this?—*evasive.*

THE SOLUTION: A GOD FACULTY?

But notice I can rationally answer, "Why wouldn't I?" for many ordinary beliefs: my belief that I see snow outside my window, my belief that I had coffee before breakfast, my belief that I have a headache, and my belief that I was born in the United States. In each of these cases, I simply find myself with the belief in question; moreover—and this is crucial—I have no good reason to doubt them. I just *find* myself with these beliefs. And I "just find" them because they were automatically triggered by an *experience*, not by any inference.

In such cases, possession is nine-tenths of the law. I would need a reason to question that I'm seeing snow. And it had better be a really good argument, one with premises stronger than my belief that I'm seeing snow over there.

Similarly for belief in God. Notice something that Saint Paul wrote in chapter 1 of Romans. He said that "since the creation of the world God's invisible qualities—his eternal power and divine nature—have been clearly seen, being understood from what has been made."

In this passage, Paul was emphasizing that everyone—Jews and non-Jews alike—naturally and unmistakably see something of God in the world. This, plus Paul's use of the visual metaphor "clearly seen," suggests a built-in tendency to believe in God, perhaps a faculty similar to sense perception in some important way. But what way? The answer Paul seems to have in mind is that there are experiences of things in the world—the grandeur of a mountain or maybe the tiny fingers of a newborn—that trigger belief in God. We just *see* something of God.

The sixteenth-century theologian John Calvin called this innate propensity to believe in God the "sense of the divine," the *sensus divinitatis*. The thirteenth-century theologian and philosopher Thomas Aquinas described it this way: we all have a predisposition to believe in God "implanted in us by nature."[3] That is, this disposition is *built into all humans* as part of their natural cognitive hardware. The *sensus divinitatis* is a belief-forming mechanism akin to memory, reason, credulity, and sense perception.

Now, it isn't that we ordinarily look at the starry hosts and reason from the belief that the universe is vast and magnificent to the conclusion that it was designed by a great and powerful intelligence. Instead, in such situations we typically just find ourselves with these beliefs about God. Similarly, a sense of guilt might also trigger the belief that there is a God to whom we are responsible. In these cases we don't run through an argument, using our observations or feelings to generate premises for the conclusion that God exists.[4]

Of course, we *could* reason that way, and we'll see later that such arguments have a place. But in general, that's not how most of us come to believe in God.

There are all manner of ordinary circumstances or experiences that trigger belief in God, or at least beliefs implying that God exists. While reading the Bible, for example, we may get the distinct impression that God is speaking to us through that passage. Or when in distress, large or small, we may ask God to protect and guide us. Alternatively, when things are going smoothly we may be struck with a palpable sense of gratitude toward God. In all these cases, the belief triggered isn't "God exists," but rather a belief that implies he does.[5] And these are the types of experiences that ordinary believers have. Nothing fancy—no visions or audible commands from on high—but no less important for their familiarity.

If this is true, then belief in God is, or can be, *basic*—produced by *experience* rather than by inference from other beliefs.

If.

WHY DOESN'T *EVERYONE* BELIEVE?

Wouldn't this so-called *sensus divinitatis*—if there *is* one—be different from our ordinary belief-forming mechanisms? Most importantly, not everyone believes in God. Whereas every properly functioning human has belief-forming mechanisms like reason, sense perception, memory, and the propensity to believe testimony, the *sensus divinitatis* doesn't appear to be part of our standard package. And if everyone does have it, a recall should be issued.

This objection is nearly right. For one thing, the Bible could not be more clear about the reality of unbelief, nor is it coy about its cause. The reason we don't all believe is the very reason for *all* our troubles:

the ravages of sin. Although—absent the presence of sin—our *sensus divinitatis* would naturally and automatically cause us to believe that God exists, sin has tragically damaged this all-important cognitive faculty. Similar to a person born blind—wholly or only partially— our natural sense of the divine no longer functions properly. In fact, a closer analogy would be the case in which someone suffers from a mental disorder, incapable of, say, discerning right from wrong: the person is gripped by a form of cognitive dysfunction, a type of insanity.[6] So, sin is an illness that affects not only what we *want*—what kinds of things we're drawn to—but also what we *think*. Our mental faculties are beset by an *intellectual* blindness; we're simply incapable of seeing things we would effortlessly see were we functioning properly.

This cognitive damage also explains why people, even among those who *do* believe, believe wildly different things. When the *sensus divinitatis* does cause belief, it doesn't always trigger belief in a personal God; perhaps the person merely believes in something "supernatural." According to Aquinas, the *sensus divinitatis* often results in

> a mixture of many errors. Some people have believed that there is no other orderer of worldly things than the celestial bodies, and so they said that the celestial bodies are gods. Other people pushed it farther, to the very elements and the things generated from them, thinking that motion and the natural function which these elements have are not present in them as the effect of some other orderer, but that other things are ordered by them.[7]

If this is right, then the *sensus divinitatis*, although widespread, doesn't generally produce belief in the God of Abraham, Isaac, and Jacob.

Nevertheless, in the history of the world—and our own time is no exception—believers (of some stripe) have greatly outnumbered unbelievers. In fact, this number may be slightly larger, including even *unbelieving scientists*. Above, Aquinas suggested that in response to the faint whispers of their damaged *sensus divinitatis*, humans might respond by positing an ultimate *natural* principle. That is, the *sensus divinitatis* might be the cause of our belief in *laws of nature*. Scientists often speak as if natural laws—like the law of gravity—*cause* objects to behave a certain way; yet natural laws, as we'll see, are merely our descriptions of the way objects behave. Perhaps this is an example of Paul's words, "They exchanged the truth of God for a lie, and worshiped and served created things rather than the Creator."[8] Like all idols, these laws might simply be placeholders for God.

Sin may also be the cause of *philosophical* skepticism, *á la* Hume and Kant. Hume, for example, was entirely right to point out that we have no good argument for an objective, physical world outside our minds. But is his further conclusion—that we aren't rational in believing in an external world—a sign that he's simply being duly cautious, demonstrating a high level of intellectual sophistication? It seems not. To doubt the existence of the book in your hands, or of the person across the dinner table from you, would be a sign that something has gone terribly wrong. In such a case, you would require professional help.[9] Of course, it wouldn't necessarily be a sign of malfunction to merely recognize that we lack noncircular arguments for the reliability of our cognitive faculties. But, in conjunction with sin, this fact sometimes causes people to question our belief-forming mechanisms altogether (including whatever mechanism is responsible for the doubt in the first place). That would explain many of philosophy's dead ends.[10]

If this is right, then atheism is similar to believing that we're hooked up to the Matrix or deep within a vivid dream from which we have yet to wake. In all such cases, the person is suffering from a serious form of cognitive malfunction. Atheism seems to be another form of madness.

HATING IT DOESN'T MAKE IT FALSE

In addition to our cognitive damage, sin causes another type of insanity. All of us frequently put ourselves before others, desiring our own glory and pleasure. This is a defect of our *wills*, a twisting of desires. In particular, we often don't *want* God to exist. Thomas Nagel, an atheist philosopher, is refreshingly candid:

I want atheism to be true and am made uneasy by the fact that some of the most intelligent and well-informed people I know are religious believers. It isn't just that I don't believe in God and, naturally, hope that I'm right in my belief. It's that I hope there is no God! I don't want there to be a God; I don't want the universe to be like that.[11]

Christopher Hitchens, both candid *and* cranky, complained,

There are . . . atheists who say that they wish the fable were truth but are unable to suspend the requisite disbelief, or have relinquished belief only with regret. To this I reply: who wishes that there was a permanent, unalterable celestial despotism that subjected us to continual surveillance and could convict us of thought-crime and who regarded us as its private property even after we died? How happy we ought to be, at the reflection that there exists not a shred of respectable evidence to support such a horrible hypothesis.[12]

And of course, he's right. Who would want a God like *that*? Seeing God through Hitchens's eyes helps us understand how Satan and his minions might view their war with God. Perhaps they see themselves as part of a bold and noble resistance against celestial tyranny. Is there any more heroic story to tell yourself while you fight in the face of certain and utter defeat? Where some people see a loving and caring father, others see a corrupt cop.

LET THE HEALING BEGIN

This is the picture then: God has created all humans with a belief-forming mechanism that generates belief in God under a wide range of ordinary circumstances. This *sensus divinitatis* is just as natural as sense perception or memory. In other words, it is innate, something we're all born with. Unfortunately, sin—that frightful disease—has badly damaged the *sensus divinitatis*. But had we not inherited this terminal illness from our parents, we would believe in God just as readily as we believe our senses, our reason, and our memory.[13] Things would be very different indeed.

This widespread cognitive damage is the result, then, of mankind's self-deception and subsequent rebellion against his creator. But God provided a way out of our dreadful condition. On his own initiative, God sent his divine son, Jesus Christ, to redeem and restore humanity through his incarnation, atonement for sin upon the cross, and resurrection to new life from the grave. Because of this divine intervention into human life, we are given a way out of our predicament and the possibility of living again in close communion with God, both here and beyond.

Moreover, God had to inform us of his offer and how we might take advantage of it. That is, he needed some way of producing in us specifically Christian beliefs, not merely belief in some god or other. And he had to do this throughout history, across a dizzying variety of cultures. Of course, God could have informed us in any number of ways, but he revealed his plan of salvation primarily in the Scriptures.[14]

But sin causes yet more problems. Just as we're blind to the glory of God declared by the heavens, our inborn infirmities—our birth defects—make us incapable of seeing the truth of these divine Scriptures. That is, in addition to our blindness to God's handiwork, neither will we naturally believe the Bible.

To repair our cognitive defects (as well as the waywardness of our affections), God's Holy Spirit gives us new life—regeneration. We are *re*generated, *re*made, *re*born. Through regeneration, God begins the gradual process of opening our eyes to his truth, beauty, and goodness. He begins to repair the *sensus divinitatis*. We begin to hear creation's testimony. Furthermore, we begin to hear Scripture's testimony: the Holy Spirit opens our hearts to the way of salvation set out in the Old and New Testaments. We come to believe the great things of the gospel, but again, not by way of any sort of inference.

The Holy Spirit acts as a type of belief-forming mechanism, immediately causing these beliefs. This work is sometimes called the "internal testimony of the Holy Spirit," and putting it this way reminds us of testimony's presence in the formation of basic beliefs.

Notice that, whereas we would have a *sensus divinitatis* even had we not fallen into sin (albeit one that worked properly), regeneration is needed only because we fell. To put it crassly, whereas the *sensus divinitatis* comes standard, the Holy Spirit's work is an aftermarket option.

TAKING STOCK

Given this Christian explanation of belief in God, we now need to return to the notions of faith and rationality. And let us give our explanation a name; let us call it the *Christian epistemic story* ("epistemic" is a three-dollar word referring to "how we know or believe").[15]

If our explanation of how most of us come to believe in God—this Christian epistemic story—is correct, or even close to correct, then belief in God can be entirely rational, even without being held on the basis of an argument. For remember our definition of rationality: *a belief is rational if it is formed by a properly functioning cognitive faculty operating in the appropriate environment.* On the Christian view of things, the *sensus divinitatis* is just such a belief-forming mechanism, a *naturally* occurring one. It will generally form beliefs closer to the truth, the less it is damaged. Some people's *sensus divinitatis* produces beliefs that are wide of the mark; in others, it is suppressed almost entirely. Humans need the work of the Holy Spirit—another belief-forming mechanism, but this time *super*natural—to intervene and begin reparations of the *sensus divinitatis.* Regeneration, then, is a supernatural fix for an otherwise natural belief-forming mechanism. In such cases then, the *sensus divinitatis* and the Holy Spirit produce rational belief in God.

But along with producing a rational belief in God, the work of the Holy Spirit simultaneously produces a rational acceptance of the gospel. Again, this belief in the great things of the gospel will be entirely rational despite not being formed by way of arguments.

Remember the circular or bootstrapping argument for our belief that we should believe the Bible. Given what we've said about the work of the Holy Spirit, we can rationally believe the Bible without needing an argument for its reliability. You read, for example, that Jesus died for your sins and you *just believe* it. It just seems right and obvious, and there's not much more you can say. Your belief that Jesus died for your sins is *basic*, just like your belief that God exists.

None of this implies that there aren't any good arguments for God's existence or for the reliability of Scripture. But these arguments won't usually result in the strength of belief we actually experience through the Holy Spirit's work (unless the Holy Spirit is working through that argument). And again, I'm not suggesting that *no one* has come to genuine Christian belief with the help of arguments. But even in such cases, it is—on the Christian view of things—the result of the Holy Spirit *working through* such arguments. On this side of the fall, genuine belief is always supernatural.

The point here is that in many cases, arguments aren't necessary for rational belief in God. If your belief in God and his gospel is the result of the Holy Spirit's work, then your belief has the default position. That is, it's up to atheists to show that it's mistaken. Just as you are within your intellectual rights to assume or take for granted that there really *is* a book in front of you, you can take belief in God for granted. And if you don't believe the gospel, yet believe in a god of some kind, this belief, too, can be rational to some degree, since it was likely formed by your *sensus divinitatis*, albeit one not dialed in.

Believing in God in this basic way is very different from believing on the basis of an argument. Moreover, believing this way is often entirely rational.

Nevertheless, arguments can become necessary, either to *defend* our belief in God or to *strengthen* it. After all, nobody's perfect.

FOR YOUR ARSENAL

- In Romans 1, the apostle Paul suggests that we naturally see God in the things that were made. Theologians have called this natural propensity—or better, this innate cognitive faculty—the *sensus divinitatis*.

- Our *sensus divinitatis*—when functioning properly or near properly—automatically triggers belief in God under a wide range of ordinary experiences. In such cases, belief in God isn't inferred but believed in the basic way.

- Sin has badly damaged our *sensus divinitatis*. This cognitive dysfunction is a form of insanity.

- In believers, the Holy Spirit has supernaturally repaired the *sensus divinitatis*, enabling it to generate belief in God in various circumstances. The Holy Spirit also enables Christians to believe the "great things of the Gospel."

- Since belief in God can be formed by a properly functioning cognitive faculty (the *sensus divinitatis*) in the appropriate environment, belief in God can be rational, even when believed in the basic way.

- *The Christian epistemic story*: the explanation of how Christians typically come to believe in God and the great things of the Gospel.

"AW, COME ON!"

{SOME OBJECTIONS}

OBJECTION 1: "THAT'S CIRCULAR!"

A theists are unlikely to be impressed by all this. One objection in particular comes to mind: Christians can't support the rationality of belief by assuming *up front* that God exists. That's too easy. After all, God's existence isn't a given in these discussions. And if God doesn't exist (and I haven't shown that he does), the whole "Christian epistemic story" never gets off the ground. A nonexistent God would have to be pretty powerful to design us with a *sensus divinitatis.*[1]

This objection is right on the mark—if we were arguing that God exists.[2] But remember that we've been responding to the objection that belief in God is *irrational*, not that it's *false*. The distinction is subtle but important. To see its importance, imagine that Richard, an atheist, has marshaled the courage to ask his Christian coworker, Alvin, about the reasonableness of belief in God:

RICHARD: Al, don't take this wrong, but how can you believe in God? I mean, given what we know today, there's simply not enough evidence to support it. At least *I've* never heard a plausible reason.

ALVIN: Well, I don't know . . . I've seen some decent arguments over the years; in any case, even if there *weren't* any good arguments, I think that belief in God can be rational. Here's one way to look at it: [Alvin tells Richard about the *sensus divinitatis* and the work of the Holy Spirit . . .]

RICHARD: Well *of course*, if God exists, then it might be rational to believe in him. But it seems fairly clear that God *doesn't* exist.

ALVIN: Why think *that*?

RICHARD: As I said before, there just isn't any evidence. None of the arguments are any good.

ALVIN: Well, I just explained how belief in God might be rational even if there *aren't* any good arguments. The "not-enough-evidence" response doesn't have much force—I've claimed that we don't usually *need* evidence.

RICHARD: And if there's no God?

ALVIN: Then belief in God isn't likely to be rational, at least if believed in the basic way. But my point is this: if God exists, then it can be rational to believe in him without an argument (because of the Christian story of belief). Now, you'll either have to argue that God doesn't exist, which would make short shrift of my claim, since the claim that belief in God can be rational if God exists obviously depends on God's existence. Or else you'll need to show me that even if God does exist, it's not rational to believe in him. For this second strategy, you'll need to argue that there's something wrong with the Christian epistemic story itself.

Again, there's an important difference between the claim that belief in God is irrational and the claim that God doesn't exist. God could exist without there being any evidence for his existence. There are surely all sorts of things that exist for which we have no evidence. So arguing that there's no evidence for God's existence doesn't show that God doesn't exist, especially if no evidence is required, as we've argued. Things aren't *that* easy for the atheist.

But notice, however, that the Christian epistemic story we told in the previous chapter doesn't settle the issue. Rather, it puts the ball in the atheist's court. We can put this as follows. We argued that

If the Christian epistemic story is true then belief in
God can be rational even apart from evidence.

Whether belief in God can be rational apart from evidence, will of course, depend on whether the Christian epistemic story is true. But is it? If atheists can cast enough doubt on the Christian epistemic story, they can block the argument. (This wouldn't, however, show that belief in God can't be rational apart from evidence, just that our particular argument doesn't work.[3]) Alvin above suggests that atheists now have two strategies for casting such doubt:

1. Argue that the Christian epistemic story has—or leads to—unacceptable problems, and therefore is (probably) not true.
2. Argue that God doesn't exist and therefore that the Christian epistemic story is (probably) not true.

If the atheist can't pull off the first strategy, then we have ruled out a common objection to belief in God, one like this:

Well, I certainly don't know whether theistic belief is *true* [that is, whether God really exists]—who could know a thing like that?—but I do know this: it is irrational, or unjustified, or not rationally justified, or contrary to reason or intellectually irresponsible.[4]

And ever since the Enlightenment, arguments against belief in God have focused on its alleged irrationality. The widespread acceptance of evidentialism encouraged doubts about the rationality of believing in God: even if it turned out that God exists, it would still be irrational to believe in him.

Of course, the second strategy is just as effective—perhaps more so. If the atheist can give us a plausible argument against God's existence, then whether it's rational to believe in God is beside the point. In addition to blocking our argument that belief in God can be rational, such an argument would settle the real issue: whether God really exists. But this second method is also much more difficult. We will turn to it in the second and third parts of the book when we consider the two most common and powerful kinds of arguments against God's existence.

But first, let's see how the atheist might execute the first strategy, option 1. We've already seen one objection in support of this strategy: the claim that by presenting the story, the Christian is arguing in a circle. It turns out that there's nothing circular about it—no bootstrapping, no question begging. We'll now consider two more objections. Later, we'll address the second, more difficult strategy, option 2, and see what sorts of arguments there are against God's existence. When we do *that*, we'll focus on the two most common (and powerful) objections, the two things that allegedly show that God doesn't exist: *science* and the existence of *evil and suffering*.

OBJECTION 2: "BELIEF IN GOD IS SHEER DOGMATISM"

But even if our use of the Christian epistemic story isn't circular, it raises other concerns. One is that if I claim that belief in God can be *basic*, I thereby stop all intelligent discussion. For if my belief in God isn't based on arguments, won't I continue believing no matter how much contrary evidence accumulates?[5] And isn't this exactly where atheists think much of the problem lies?

Sam Harris says that "religious faith is the one species of human ignorance that will not admit of even the possibility of correction."[6] And atheist Penn Jillette, one-half of the illusionist/comedy team of Penn & Teller says this: "I don't travel in circles where people say, 'I have faith, I believe this in my heart and nothing you can say or do can shake my faith.' That's just a long-winded religious way to say, 'shut up.'"[7]

This is a familiar grievance. Isn't basic belief in God simply a form of blind dogmatism?

I don't see why it has to be. Just because I form a belief without an argument, that doesn't mean the belief will be immune to arguments. After all, many uncontroversial basic beliefs succumb to arguments. Imagine that you're driving through the rolling country and see what looks like a sheep on the far hill and automatically find yourself with the belief that there's a sheep. When you stop at the local diner, however, your waitress tells you that there aren't any sheep in this part of the country, although there's a sheepdog that looks just like a sheep from a distance and this is probably what you saw. Now, you initially believed that there was a sheep on the hill in the basic way, without any inference. But given the waitress's revelation, you no longer believe that you saw a sheep. You have had your mind changed despite having formed your initial belief in the basic way.[8] Your belief wasn't immune to argument at all.

Suppose I come to believe that God exists in the basic way—say, because it's what my parents taught me, or I just witnessed the birth of my first child. But I'm eventually beset by doubts—I've read too much Christopher Hitchens, way too carelessly. Suppose that Hitchens's arguments seem to be full of piercing insights, and now that I'm privy to these insights, I can't comfortably continue believing Hitchens *and* that God exists. Something has to change. If Hitchens's revelations are powerful enough, perhaps I'll give up belief in God. Or maybe I should read some Plantinga.

Whatever the case, arguments can dislodge belief in God. Belief in God, in other words, isn't immune to what we might call *defeaters*, arguments that provide enough evidence to overthrow or defeat your initial belief. Yet my belief in God may survive defeaters if those defeaters can themselves be defeated (call these counterarguments "defeater-defeaters"). So the second objection—that the Christian epistemic story implies that we can stubbornly cling to belief in God in the face of overwhelming contrary evidence—has little going for it.[9]

OBJECTION 3: "ANYTHING GOES"

But even so, if belief in God needs no argument, it still seems that we leave the door open to all sorts of nutty claims. This is known as the "Great Pumpkin Objection": Couldn't someone, asks Plantinga, believe that the Great Pumpkin returns every Halloween and defend this belief by claiming that he believes it in the basic way? [10]

How can Christians now exclude other beliefs—no matter how crazy—without being accused of discrimination? To put it differently, a Christian who claims that belief in God is basic seems intellectually promiscuous.

Now why would the Christian epistemic story open the flood-gates of goofiness? After all, atheists and believers alike believe many things in the basic way—their names, for example. *This* basic belief doesn't result in an "anything goes" policy, so why then would belief in God? It must be that the objector thinks there's something importantly similar between belief in God and belief in the Great Pumpkin.

But what might the similarity be? Overall, God and the Great Pumpkin have very different skill sets. They don't seem anything alike. Furthermore, Christians have a plausible story of how belief in God is rationally formed, whereas there's no such story for the Great Pumpkin.[11] The assumption that they're relevantly similar seems little more than a tacit assumption of the very thing that the atheist must argue for. That is, the common characteristic that allows the comparison seems to be that neither exists (or that there's no evidence for either, or that both require evidence). Without these or some similar assumptions, the Great Pumpkin Objection doesn't work. But of course, the atheist can't simply assume that God doesn't exist or that there's no evidence or that we need evidence. These are controversial claims, things that would need to be argued for.

A BENEFIT: CREATING JOBS FOR ATHEISTS

Remember that Alvin above conceded that if God doesn't exist, our explanation of Christian faith is probably false. But this seems little more than a statement of the obvious. If God doesn't exist, who cares if the explanation is bogus? And who cares if belief in God—by some astronomical fluke—turned out to be rational? If the atheist could show that God doesn't exist, we can all go home. Game over.

Well, perhaps, *if* the atheist could do this. But that's a sizeable *if*, which is part of the point. Because our Christian epistemic story seems to survive some strong objections, the atheist must now argue for the proposition that *God doesn't exist*. Atheists can't merely sit back and ask us to prove that God exists before they deem us rational. Although that would be an enviable polemical position, one requiring very little heavy lifting, they now have a job to do.

So then, the burden of proof is now on the atheists. This point is almost important enough to tattoo it somewhere.

ANOTHER BENEFIT: FAITH FINDING UNDERSTANDING

The Christian epistemic story can also help Christians *understand* their own faith, not merely defend it. It puts things in perspective. After all, if—like most of us living downstream of the Enlightenment— they hear the siren song of evidentialism, they might worry over the fact that they don't have such support, and neither do most believers they know. Yet if there's a plausible explanation for how they *in fact* believe, an explanation that matches their own experience, then they can stop worrying and focus on more important things. Most believers have better things to do than rummage around for arguments supporting God's existence.

Of course, the Christian epistemic story can certainly help believers defend themselves. We saw this in the conversation between Alvin and Richard. After a believer explains the Christian epistemic story to an unbeliever, the conversation will probably turn quickly to the question of whether God exists. In this way, having the Christian epistemic story in hand helps direct and focus the discussion.

So we have a plausible explanation of how a believer might rationally believe in God despite having no arguments for that belief. According to this explanation, however, belief in God isn't arbitrary, with no legitimate ground or cause. It receives its support from experience.

We have, therefore, removed one type of argument against religious belief, one demanding that all believers base their belief in God on an argument. We've seen that such a complaint has little leverage, given our Christian epistemic story. Unless of course, there is no God.

But why think a thing like that? Are there any good arguments for it? Any against it? It's time to look more closely at arguments.

FOR YOUR ARSENAL

- One objection to the Christian epistemic story is that it's circular: that it presupposes that God exists. This objection fails because the Christian epistemic story isn't offered as a reason or evidence for believing that *God exists*, but as an explanation of how *belief in God can be rational*. The atheist must now show that the Christian epistemic story is (probably) not true.

- There are two main ways the atheist can try to show that the Christian epistemic story is (probably) not true: (1) Argue that there are problems with the Christian epistemic story. (2) Argue that God doesn't exist.

- The three objections of this chapter are examples of the first strategy; the second strategy is dealt with in Parts 2 and 3 below.

- *Defeaters*: arguments that provide enough evidence to overthrow or defeat your belief in God.

- A second objection to the Christian epistemic story— another example of the first strategy—is that, by believing in God in the basic way, belief in God will be immune to *defeaters*. But believing something in the basic way doesn't imply that it will be immune to defeaters; many of our ordinary basic beliefs are susceptible to revision.

- A third objection to the Christian epistemic story—also an example of the first strategy—is that, by allowing for belief in God to be basic, we would open the door to beliefs that are clearly irrational. But our ordinary basic beliefs don't open the floodgates to silliness, so why should belief in God?

- The Christian epistemic story provides important benefits: it puts the burden of proof on the atheist while providing Christians with a proper understanding of their own belief in God.

INTERMISSION

The Art of Self-Defense

8

LET'S BE REALISTIC

WHAT MAKES AN ARGUMENT GOOD?

Remember that the evidentialist objection has two parts. The first is that *to be rational, a belief must be supported by sufficient evidence.* This is evidentialism proper and—even though it's false—most Christians have accepted it since the Enlightenment. The second part to the evidentialist objection—the objection part—is that *there is little or no evidence for God's existence.* Is this part true? There are, after all, many arguments for God's existence. Why think that none of these are any good?

Not surprisingly, it depends on what we mean by *good.* But—and this *does* surprise people—our standards for arguments are much more than a matter of logic. (But not less.) When someone thinks that your argument leaves something to be desired, is there an agreed-upon rulebook to which you can both refer? Isn't the other person a bit too biased to pass judgment on an argument against *his* position? Isn't there a conflict of interests? How do we decide who wins an argument and whether or not the rules have been flouted?

These are very good questions.

CLUES, NOT PROOFS

When it comes to arguing for God, Plantinga immediately concedes that he sees no way to conclusively prove that God exists. This, however, shouldn't bother Christians. After all, Plantinga points out, "very little of what we believe can be 'demonstrated' or 'shown' in the sense of an irrefutable proof."[1] This goes for atheism, as well as for our belief in physical objects outside our minds, and our belief that the world has existed for more than five minutes. We saw ample evidence of this earlier.

So, very few arguments are unassailable, and the sooner we disavow ourselves of this impossible standard, the better. We never encounter the kinds of airtight arguments we find in mathematics. Provided we're willing to make the necessary concessions and contortions, we can always avoid an argument's conclusion. Sometimes these contortions become extremely uncomfortable. The invention of quantum logic, for example, is an attempt to change the very laws of logic, to make logic conform to our latest science. Even mathematicians have campaigned to strike the law of the excluded middle from their books.[2] Is nothing sacred?

None of this means that arguments don't provide important evidential support for many of our beliefs. Nor does it mean that there aren't arguments that support belief in God. In a famous but long-unpublished paper titled "Two Dozen (or so) Theistic Arguments," Plantinga sketches a wide variety of arguments that—if carefully developed—provide excellent evidence for God's existence.[3] But he makes it clear that "these arguments are not coercive in the sense that every person is obliged to accept their premises on pain of irrationality."[4] Rather, it may be merely that "some or many sensible people do accept their premises."[5]

It's helpful to think about arguments for (and against) God's existence as providing *clues* rather than proofs.[6] A clue isn't usually irrefutable evidence for some conclusion, but rather, it points toward a conclusion, suggesting one possibility over others. And even though there is almost always some uncertainty about where clues point, they still objectively restrict the options. Clues aren't compatible with just any old situation; otherwise they wouldn't be clues. Clues have to clue us in, lead us down a specific path.

The notion of clues reminds us of detective stories. But the type of reasoning used by Sherlock Holmes isn't restricted to whodunits. Science traffics in clues rather than proofs. Physicist Stephen Hawking, when discussing the origins of the universe, says, for example, "Astronomers have also found other *fingerprints* supporting the big bang picture of a hot, tiny early universe."[7] Fingerprints aren't a cause, but merely a link to it—a guide.

There's little mystery why we find the search for clues in science: this search runs through all reasoning. Yet science gives us some of the best examples. Philosophers call the method for finding clues *inference to the best explanation*. And because we use this kind of argument for nearly everything, we can, by looking at science, extract general lessons for how we argue for and against God.

Inference to the best explanation works like this: You gather facts and then—given these facts (and other things you already know about the world)—you shop for the best explanation of the facts. And, to keep things interesting, there will usually be many possible explanations for your shopping pleasure (theoretically, there will be infinitely many). And as recent philosophers and historians of science have shown, a lot more goes into choosing an explanation than logic and observation. Many other factors come into play, including how simple the theory is and how well it conforms to beliefs we already hold.

An example will make it clearer.

THE WORLD'S BEST EXAMPLE

In the 1500s, the Polish cleric and astronomer Nicolaus Copernicus proposed that the earth moves around the sun rather than vice versa. And during the ensuing debate over a sun-centered universe ("helio-centricity") and an earth-centered one ("geocentricity"), both sides had available the same observational data, the same facts. The actual debate was over which theory *best explained* the data everyone was privy to.

But if everyone was privy to all the same information, why was there disagreement? It wasn't that one side had more intelligence. Rather, part of the reason is that agreed-upon facts are always subject to more than one explanation. William E. Carroll of Oxford illustrates this with a story about the twentieth-century philosopher Ludwig Wittgenstein.

> Wittgenstein once asked a friend, "Tell me, why do people always say it was natural for man to assume that the Sun went round the Earth rather than that the Earth was rotating?" His friend replied, "Well, obviously, because it just *looks* as though the Sun is going round the Earth." To which Wittgenstein responded, "Well, what would it have looked like if it had looked as though the Earth was rotating?"[8]

Well, *exactly* the same. Given only our ordinary, unaided observations from the earth, the universe looks identical in a heliocentric and a geo-centric universe. Yet these are two very different universes. And even today, no one has *observed* the earth moving around the sun. Of course, that doesn't mean it doesn't. Nevertheless, there are multiple ways to make your theory—to make what you *think*—agree with what you *see*.

A MATTER OF PERSPECTIVE

Notice then that for most debates in science, the data—the observa-tions—are the same for both sides. The interpretation of the observations is different. And it's often very difficult to see the plausibility of another interpretation—or even that there *is* another interpretation—from the vantage of your current interpretation. Wittgenstein was fond of pointing to the famous "duck-rabbit" drawing, in which *you* might see a rabbit, while someone else sees a duck. It can take quite a bit of effort for you to make the internal shift to see the duck. Yet once you see the duck, you wonder why you didn't see it earlier. This is what happened in the shift from geocentricism to heliocentrism. One historian of science called this shift "picking up the other end of the stick."[9]

All of this might be seen as a way of merely saying that we can't ever be 100 percent logically certain that an explanation is the correct one. But a lack of logical certainty isn't the only source of disagreement; another factor is that no two people share exactly the same perspective of the world. No one but you has ever looked through your eyes. You are one of a kind, a beautiful and unique snowflake.

The person who has probably done the most to help us see the importance of perspective in scientific reasoning (and therefore in all reasoning) is the famous historian of science Thomas Kuhn. Kuhn's wildly popular book, *The Structure of Scientific Revolutions*—first published in the 1960s—played an important role in the demise of logical positivism. In particular, Kuhn refuted the prevailing view that science proceeds neatly by pure reason acting on sentences describing direct observation. The paradigmatic cases of scientific "advancement" didn't proceed merely by way of a simple methodological recipe.

OLD BELIEFS CONTROL NEW BELIEFS

Kuhn and others pointed out that when it comes to choosing a hypothesis that accords with observations, the beliefs you bring to the choice will affect the choice. Copernicus, for example, believed that the sun is a representation of God and so deserves to be at the center of the universe. Kepler and Galileo believed something similar. Einstein, to take another example, resisted quantum mechanics, with its fundamental uncertainty and capriciousness, because he believed that God "doesn't play dice." A scientist's previous beliefs will dictate—often implicitly—the range of hypotheses he or she thinks is plausible.

And this is true for every scientist. At least for the human ones. All scientists come to science having fundamental philosophical views about reality, knowledge, and values. This isn't necessarily bad, but it *is* necessary.

Consider the general case where two people are debating the virtues of their respective scientific theories. The person with the first theory must advertise the virtues of his theory, all the while believing the theory. No surprise there. But often, what counts as a virtue will depend on the theory itself. Similarly for the person arguing for the competing theory. Each side may want or value different things. If, for example, I believe Newtonian physics and you believe Einstein's theory of relativity, we may both argue that our respective theory better explains the nature of space. But the nature of space itself—of what counts as space—is dictated by the theories, and so will affect our views of what counts as a virtue.

We have to stand somewhere while arguing; we always argue from some vantage point, from some perspective. In Thomas Nagel's words, there's no "view from nowhere." And when arguing about the vantage point (the scientific theory, for example), you must stand on the very thing for which you're arguing. There will, of course, be overlapping beliefs for any two worldviews, and it is in this area of overlap that arguments gain traction. Whenever discussing anything with anyone, there must be some common ground. But some of the ground is altogether uncommon.

And the more fundamental the belief for which you're arguing, the more entrenched it can be. Beliefs can become so ingrained that we forget that they might be false. They are sometimes only "obvious" to us because they are ours. Kuhn pointed out that "Newton's second law of motion [$F = ma$] . . . took centuries of difficult factual and theoretical research to achieve, [but it] behaves for those committed to Newton's theory very much like a purely logical statement that no amount of observation could refute."[10] Moreover, the more deeply a view is ingrained, the less likely we will see it as influencing us—or see it at all. If you want to know what water is, don't ask the fish.

BELIEVING IS SEEING—AND *NOT* SEEING

Even direct observation can vary from person to person. Kuhn calls our attention to the experimental literature that suggests, "What a man sees depends both upon what he looks at and also upon what his previous visual-conceptual experience has taught him to see."[11] One of his examples borders on unbelievable, an experiment performed at the Hanover Institute:

> An experimental subject who puts on goggles fitted with invert-ing lenses initially sees the entire world upside down. At the start his perceptual apparatus functions as it had been trained to function in the absence of the goggles, and the result is extreme disorientation, an acute personal crisis. But after the subject has begun to learn to deal with his new world, his entire visual field flips over, usually after an intervening period in which vision is simply confused. Thereafter, objects are again seen as they had been before the goggles were put on.[12]

There is, then, a wholesale switch from one view of the world to another, with an intervening period of crisis or uneasiness. So, whereas the duck-rabbit picture "shows that two men with the same retinal impressions can see different things; the inverting lenses show that two men with different retinal images can see the same thing."[13]

In both cases, we see that sense perception depends on what a person brings to the observation. Of course, that doesn't mean that *anything* goes, but it does show that subjectivity turns up in surprising places.

Our previous beliefs can even determine *whether* we'll observe something, not just *how*. Before Copernicus, Western scientists believed that the heavens are immutable—that they never change. Given this immutability, there could be no new stars, no novae. And so Kuhn asked,

> Can it conceivably be an accident, for example, that Western astronomers first saw changes [e.g., new stars or novae] in the previously immutable heavens during the half-century after Copernicus's new paradigm was first proposed? The Chinese, whose cosmological beliefs did not preclude celestial change, had recorded the appearance of many new stars in the heavens at a much earlier date. Also, even without the aid of a telescope, the Chinese had systematically recorded the appearance of sunspots centuries before they were seen by Galileo and his contemporaries.[14]

In such cases, we don't have merely a different interpretation of the same observations, but different observations altogether.

Science, then—like everything we do—has a human face. It never floats free of the desires, cares, and propensities of individual *people*. But this built-in subjectivity goes against everything we think we know about science. Unbelievers—from David Hume to the logical positivists to Christopher Hitchens—have exalted science as the paragon of cool, objective reason. And to be sure, science is a superb way to study the universe. But the reality of how scientists actually do their remarkable work is more complex than the naïve Enlightenment view that most atheists cling to. And on their view, science would be a lot easier. If science were really as simple as the Enlightenment believed, science would be a lot easier, and we'd already have jet packs.

SACRED COW TIPPING

Not everyone is happy with Kuhn's findings. Sam Harris, for example, complains that "many unwary consumers of these ideas have concluded that science is just another area of human discourse and, as such, is not more anchored to the facts of this world than literature or religion are. All truths are up for grabs."[15]

Harris is right: anyone who reads Kuhn and thinks that "all truths are up for grabs" has indeed been unwary. (And the fact that Kuhn's book is the most cited of the twentieth century suggests that more people are referring to the book than have a right to.) Incautious readings of Kuhn have fueled the postmodern fire, fanning its flames of relativism and other silliness.

But I suspect that much of the secular resistance to Kuhn— Harris's included—is in response not to incautious readings of his book, but to sober ones. History has shown that science simply isn't as logically pristine as we once thought. It turns out that science really is "just another area of human discourse."

Another reason for secular resistance to Kuhn is that he compares changes in scientific theory to religious conversions. "The transfer of allegiance," said Kuhn, "from paradigm to paradigm is a conversion experience that cannot be forced."[16] After the conversion, "Scientists then often speak of the 'scales falling from the eyes' or of the 'lightning flash' that 'inundates' a previously obscure puzzle."[17]

But a scientist's resistance to a new theory can be insurmountable, regardless of the evidence. The physicist Max Planck bitterly remarked that "a new scientific truth does not triumph by convincing its opponents and making them see the light, but rather because its opponents eventually die, and a new generation grows up that is familiar with it."[18]

To add insult to injury, no doubt unintentionally, Kuhn said that in many respects the closest "creative pursuit" to science is theology.[19] Science *and* religion are ways of understanding reality. But for science-oriented atheists, science has to pull double duty, performing functions similar to those of religion.

WHAT'S THE POINT?

The "humanity" of science doesn't at all exclude objectivity. But recognizing its subjectivity allows us to approach the subject with our eyes open, rather than with our heads in the sand. Being a Pollyanna is just as bad as being a pessimist. The point isn't that we should embrace relativism with respect to worldviews. Nor does a lack of certainty mean that one view can't be more rational than another. But your beliefs about reality—including what you think humans are like—will determine how you judge an argument's success. They will determine what you consider to be a good argument.

Reasoning in real life—science included—is extremely complicated, and we can't artificially distill it to a neat and simple method. Scientists reason the same way all humans must: from a limited perspective that shapes their decisions.

The importance of perspective slowly snuck up on me during my graduate study of philosophy. Frequently, I saw philosophers of equal brilliance carefully consider all the same arguments, yet end up on opposite sides of an issue, each entirely convinced he or she was right. Philosophy has a human face too.

The point is this: we should expect that the beliefs we already have about God will affect our attitude toward arguments for and against God's existence. The credibility of belief in God will depend often on very personal things. Tim Keller points out:

> If you have known many wise, loving, kind, and insightful Christians over the years, and if you have seen churches that are devout in belief yet civic-minded and generous, you will find the intellectual case for Christianity much more plausible. If, on the other hand, the preponderance of your experience is with nominal Christians (who bear the name but don't practice it) or with self-righteous fanatics, then the arguments for Christianity will have to be extremely strong for you to concede that they have any cogency at all.[20]

Again, more goes into evaluating arguments than our beliefs and the logical relations between them. Our emotions and desires, our likes and dislikes, often influence which new beliefs we're willing to take on.

And, whether God exists or not, the answer matters. Even the person who claims to have no opinion about God has for years made implicit choices in accord with one answer or the other. The centrality of the question is why many of us care so deeply about it. And both sides care. The atheist Thomas Nagel says, "I am curious whether there is anyone who is genuinely indifferent as to whether there is a God—anyone who, whatever his actual belief about the matter, doesn't particularly want either one of the answers to be correct."[21]

For better or worse, this is the way it is: humans don't enter debates as detached and disinterested inquirers. We saw earlier that Nagel and Hitchens want atheism to be true, just as I want Christianity to be true.

So let's not kid ourselves. We all come to arguments for and against God having a stake, and at some level knowing that these stakes are high. And because we already have opinions about religion, the arguments are going to seem more or less plausible given these opinions. Just as in science, what we think the world is like will determine what premises and conclusions we think are likely. An atheist is going to be naturally predisposed to think that there is something wrong (somewhere) with arguments that conclude *God exists*. The theist, on the other hand, will probably think such arguments are more plausible, all things being equal. To put it generally, you'll be more inclined to accept arguments for things you already strongly believe.

This doesn't mean we'll think every argument with our preferred conclusion is a good one—or even a plausible one. I recognize that there are bad arguments for God's existence. It's not as if our predispositions make us entirely blind to the force of the opposing view. But to ignore the reality of the situation is naïve at best.

So let's be realistic, shall we?[22]

FOR YOUR ARSENAL

- A good argument need not be irrefutable. In fact, very little of what we believe can be argued for in this way. The conclusion for nearly any argument can be avoided by someone who is willing to make the necessary concessions.

- Rather than an irrefutable proof for (or against) God's existence, we should, at best, expect arguments that provide clues—arguments that, although not irrefutable, make the conclusion plausible.

- Old beliefs control new beliefs. When inferring which explanation best explains some phenomena, our current beliefs—the beliefs we come to the inference with—will influence what we consider to be the best explanation.

- Not only do our current beliefs affect which new beliefs we'll accept, but so do our emotions and desires, our likes and dislikes.

- The subjectivity of reasoning in real life doesn't imply that "anything goes." There are still objective standards to which we can appeal. By recognizing the subjective factors, we can better control how they influence our reasoning.

STARTING AN ARGUMENT

BELIEF IN GOD: THE DEFAULT POSITION

E arlier we saw that, in many cases, we can *begin* with belief in God—we can believe in him without arguing to him. That is, the burden of proof is on atheists to give us a good reason to question God's existence. Like belief that there's a tree there, or that your mom *is* your mom, belief in God can be legitimately (i.e., rationally) taken as the default position.

But we also saw that basic belief in God isn't immune to objections; potential defeaters abound. In fact, most Christians in the West now encounter potential defeaters for belief in God, arguments against God's existence that are powerful enough to get their attention. The late Catholic philosopher Philip Quinn went so far as to say that "many, perhaps most, intellectually sophisticated adults in our culture are seldom if ever in conditions which are right for [belief in God] to be properly basic for them."[1]

Maybe our believing predecessors got through life without so much as stepping in an argument, but not our generation, not now. We live in a time where large swaths of our culture encounter objections to their belief in God, some of them vexing. Even though belief in God can legitimately be the default position, that position can be contested. Then it becomes necessary to protect our faith.

And when arguments come into play, we can no longer merely assume—for those arguments—that God exists. After all, that's the very thing the other person is questioning.

BLOCKING ATTACKS, FORTIFYING POSITIONS, AND ATTACKING ENEMY OUTPOSTS

Christians can use arguments in at least three ways with respect to belief in God. First, when we're confronted with a potential defeater—an argument that assaults the bastion of belief—we can use counterarguments to defend our belief in God. We can, that is, parry or block the attack. Second, we can also use arguments to strengthen our belief in God, even if there's no defeater in sight. It might be prudent to make the walls sturdier. And third, we can go on the offensive, providing potential defeaters for atheism. We can think of this as launching an assault on enemy outposts.

Of course, sometimes the best defense is a good offense. Other times, vice versa. And often a single argument performs more than just one task, pulling double (or triple) duty.

Notice that the believer can provide an argument for, say, God's existence without actually basing her own belief on that argument. Suppose a Christian points to the apparent design of biological organisms, arguing that the best explanation for this appearance is that these organisms really were designed. This type of argument can be powerful, yet the Christian's belief in God need not be based on it. Nevertheless, such an argument can certainly strengthen her belief in

God, further confirming her already vibrant faith. But merely dealing in arguments doesn't necessarily mean you have capitulated to evidentialism.

INVISIBLE ASSUMPTIONS

Remember that every argument begins with assumptions. And because, as Aristotle said, "Well begun is half done,"[2] many arguments are won or lost on assumptions. We need to know which assumptions are legitimate and which aren't. We need to know how to start an argument.

One of the troubles is that an argument requires so many assumptions that most of them go unnoticed. We've already seen that we nearly always assume that the laws of logic are reliable, or that there's a physical world outside our mind, or that the person to whom we're talking has thoughts and feelings similar to our own. But sometimes we make illegitimate assumptions, things that shouldn't be taken for granted. And it's usually difficult to detect these illicit assumptions. The undesirables get in by keeping their heads down.

To make things more confusing, the list of *verboten* assumptions changes with the context, depending on who's arguing for what, and with whom. If, for example, I tell a pro-choice advocate that abortion is wrong because murder is wrong, the pro-choice proponent would be right to think that I'm sneaking in something along the way, assuming something that can't—in this context—rightly be assumed. He's entirely willing to allow the premise *Murder is wrong*, but there's at least one other important premise that I failed to mention, namely, *Abortion is murder*. But of course, that's really the issue, isn't it? *Is* abortion murder? By assuming up front that it is, I make things altogether too easy for myself.

Of course, there are other situations where it wouldn't be a problem to assume that abortion is murder. Suppose two people are attending a pro-life rally, and they're debating what sorts of legislation should be put in place to end abortion. It's tolerably clear that in this context they can take for granted that abortion is murder—they probably both agree that it is.

We import illicit assumptions so readily because we often argue for things we deeply care about. Our eyes are fixed on the conclusion rather than on the path to it. Moreover, these issues usually depend on more fundamental beliefs, beliefs so natural (to us) that they have become invisible.

TAKING ATHEISM FOR GRANTED

Notice then, that when a Christian argues for God's existence, she cannot import her own belief in God into the argument, using—even implicitly—*God exists* as a premise. This doesn't mean that she doesn't, herself, believe in God while she's presenting her argument. Nor does it mean that she must base her own belief on the argument she's currently employing. Rather, she should simply avoid arguing in a circle. The argument need have nothing to do with her own belief.

And neither can the atheist—when arguing against God's existence—take his atheism for granted. Again, this doesn't mean that he must refrain from believing that God doesn't exist; it merely means that he should resist the temptation to use his atheism as a premise in certain arguments. Again, no circles.

This is easier said than done. Recall the earlier claim—made by Richard Dawkins and Nicholas Humphrey—that a religious upbringing is a type of child abuse. When Humphrey, for example, demands that believers refrain from addling the minds of their children with religious nonsense, behind such a demand is the belief that there's no God. After all, if he thought Christians were teaching children the sober truth, he wouldn't call it nonsense. Yet Humphrey skips over *arguing* that God doesn't exist and rushes right into expressing his moral indignation.

This isn't an isolated case. When people condemn religious faith as foolish or absurd, they often assume up front that it's false. For example, when Marx criticized religion as the opiate of the people or when Freud complained that belief in God is wish fulfillment, they were both implicitly assuming that God doesn't exist. Yet they didn't explicitly argue for it; they simply helped themselves.

Now, believers can agree that religion has been misused to control people, and that many of us do take comfort in a heavenly Father—all the while believing in God. In themselves, these aren't reasons against God's existence. But if Freud had shown us that belief in God is *mere* wish fulfillment because there's no God, then he would have had a point.

I don't know whether Marx and Freud realized what they were doing. But many atheists are happily aware that they take atheism for granted and do so as a principle or rule of argumentation. The late Antony Flew claimed that, in the debate between believer and unbeliever, unbelief is the legitimate place to begin, a rule he called "the presumption of atheism." (I need to immediately add that Flew gave up his ardent lifelong atheism near the end of his life.) Flew said that the burden of proof "must lie upon the theist"; it's up to the Christian to provide evidence for God's existence and not with the atheist to show that there is no God.[3] And if the theist can't provide the requisite evidence, then we have all the evidence we need that there is no God—namely none. This is quite the bargain for atheists: justification by faith alone.

But why should we think that there's such a thing as the presumption of atheism? We find a clue in a comment by atheist Michael Scriven: "The proper alternative, where there is no evidence, is not suspension of belief, e.g., about Santa Claus; it is *disbelief.*"[4] To put it generally, absence of evidence is evidence of absence.

Scriven claims that Santa Claus is relevantly similar to God, presumably in that neither exists, and that there's scanty evidence for both. But it's difficult to see how this is anything more than justifying the presumption of atheism by presuming atheism.[5]

We saw the same move in the Great Pumpkin Objection. And once you see the pattern, you find it everywhere. Here's Sam Harris's variation:

> To see how much our culture currently partakes of the irrationality of our enemies, just substitute the name of your favorite Olympian

for "God" wherever this word appears in public discourse. Imagine President Bush addressing the National Prayer Breakfast in these terms: "Behind all of life and all history there is a dedication and a purpose, set by the hand of a just and faithful Zeus."[6]

When you substitute "Zeus" for "God" that *does* sound crazy. It also sounds crazy when you replace "God" with "zebra" in that sentence. (This is like Mad Libs.) Richard Dawkins, too, enjoys this sort of game: "I have found it an amusing strategy, when asked whether I am an atheist, to point out that the questioner is also an atheist when considering Zeus, Apollo, Amon Ra, Mithras, Baal, Thor, Wotan, the Golden Calf and the Flying Spaghetti Monster. I just go one god further."[7] Dawkins's strategy (to say it again) is to establish an analogy between God and something no one today would admit believing in. Daniel Dennett's employment of this strategy, by the way, replaces God with Superman.[8]

To be fair, though, if there *were* such an analogy between God and these whimsical creatures, then these atheists would be on to something.

But that's the question, isn't it?

FOR YOUR ARSENAL

- Even though belief in God—like your belief that there's a chair in front of you—can be held in the basic way, there are times when it can be legitimately challenged by an argument, by a potential defeater.

- With respect to belief in God, Christians can use arguments in three main ways: (1) to defend their belief in God against potential defeaters; (2) to strengthen or buttress their own belief in God; and (3) to argue against atheism, that is, to present potential defeaters for atheism.

- Because we are often unaware of our tacit assumptions—of things we readily take for granted—we need to take great care not to assume the very thing for which we're arguing. This gets more difficult the more fundamental the topic is.

- Many contemporary arguments against God's existence implicitly assume that God doesn't exist or that belief in God is irrational, comparing God with the Great Pumpkin, Zeus, Superman, or the Flying Spaghetti Monster.

10

LAW AND ORDER

THE NEXT STEP:
DEALING WITH DEFEATERS

Christians can ordinarily take God's existence for granted, without having an argument for it. God has designed us to believe in him as automatically as I believe that I had eggs for breakfast this morning. Belief in God is the default position for creatures like us.

This default belief, however, is very different from assuming that God exists in an argument with an unbeliever. It has nothing to do with arguments. Yet it's usually not long before we're confronted with arguments that run contrary to belief in God. Soon enough our position is attacked (while we were going about our own business). When such attacks occur, we'll need to defend ourselves and perhaps others nearby. It's time to become acquainted with some arguments.

These arguments can be powerful even if not foolproof. On both sides. Yet you need not have *all* the answers, just the most strategic ones. So in the rest of the book, we'll consider the two most common and powerful attacks on belief in God:

- Science has shown that God doesn't exist.
- Evil and suffering show that God doesn't exist.

And at this point, you have an excellent head start. Our discussion of faith, evidence, and arguments has given you a distinct advantage. When in the grip of evidentialism, Christians are stuck defending themselves with both hands tied, caught in fruitless, frustrating quagmires. More than that, if they don't know that faith is legitimately a *natural* stance, they'll employ the wrong strategy—while adopting the wrong attitude. Frantically seeking permission to believe in God isn't the same as calmly defending properly grounded faith.

It's now time to round out your arsenal by considering specific arguments, arguments that aren't mere philosophical subtleties, but are at the center of today's conflict.

"THE STARRY HEAVENS ABOVE AND THE MORAL LAW WITHIN"

Immanuel Kant was the Enlightenment thinker *par excellence*. His influence—for better or worse—would be difficult to overstate.[1] This is surprising, because his writing is some of the most impenetrable in all of Western history. It's probably *why* he's so influential.[2] But Kant had his moments. Here's one of his most memorable and lucid utterances: "Two things fill the mind with ever new and increasing admiration and reverence, the more frequently and persistently one's meditation deals with them: the starry heavens above me and the moral law within me."[3]

It's no coincidence that the two potential defeaters we'll consider correspond to the very things that filled Kant's mind with admiration and awe. In both cases, the topics congregate around the nature of a *moral law* and the *natural order* of the universe—law and order.

We need not go very far to seek the reason.

"THE STARRY HEAVENS ABOVE"

Recall our discussion of mankind's built-in cognitive faculties. According to Christianity, God has designed us with a natural faculty that causes us to believe in him under a wide variety of ordinary experiences—the *sensus divinitatis*. Many of these ordinary experiences come from our interactions with creation itself. We saw this suggested by Paul in Romans 1 ("since the creation of the world God's invisible qualities—his eternal power and divine nature—have been clearly seen, being understood from what has been made"). Psalm 19, too, suggests a *sensus divinitatis*.

> *The heavens declare the glory of God;*
> *the skies proclaim the work of his hands.*
> *Day after day they pour forth speech;*
> *night after night they display knowledge.*
> *There is no speech or language*
> *where their voice is not heard.*
> *Their voice goes out into all the earth,*
> *their words to the ends of the world.*[4]

The heavens provide a type of *testimony* that can trigger knowledge of God. God's handiwork resonates with us, not just making us feel all tingly, but causing us to recognize, in some way or other, God's glory (and therefore his existence).

Not surprisingly, then, humans are built with an irresistible desire to understand creation. And because science is one of the ways we interact with God's handiwork—an imminently impressive way—scientific knowledge figures large in the debate over God's existence. Science and the knowledge of God are inevitably linked.

In a rather ironic twist, the *sensus divinitatis*—despite being an "argument-free" mechanism—influences the results of arguments for God's existence. Our tendency to see God through "what has been made" makes arguments from nature so powerful: they tend to resonate with people to the extent that their *sensus divinitatis* is functioning properly. So, these arguments cut with the grain. If the order and complexity of creation have caused me to believe in God by way of the *sensus divinitatis*, I'll probably think arguments employing this order and complexity are better than I would have otherwise.

As an aside, Romans 1 and Psalm 19 have traditionally been used to support "natural theology," the practice of *arguing* for God's existence without reliance on Scripture. But I think this use misses the point of these passages—they say nothing at all about arguments. Instead, they use the metaphors of sense perception and testimony. Nature just *shows* us God's glory; we just *see* God's attributes. Arguments are the least of it.

In any case, our natural tendency to see God in creation helps explain why arguments from science have figured prominently in the battle between belief and unbelief. We see this more today than ever in the writings of contemporary atheists. They can't help it. And we can't blame them.

"THE MORAL LAW WITHIN"

But ethics and morality—good and evil, right and wrong—are as important as creation. If anything is apparent in the writings of the new atheists, it's the moral indignation that soaks the pages. On the one hand, atheists are incensed by religious believers' frequent and obvious moral failures. On the other hand, they complain when believers do just what their religion tells them to, like believing in a God that sends people to hell. Believers, too, are apparently damned, whether they do or don't. Jesus, in a moment of underappreciated sarcasm, rightly characterized this generation:

> *We played the flute for you,*
> *and you did not dance;*
> *we sang a dirge,*
> *and you did not mourn.*[5]

In any case, many of the atheists' grievances are moral ones, founded upon an acute sense of ethical superiority. Very few things focus an issue like our God-given sense of morality.

And this "God-givenness" of morality is exactly why it's central to these debates. Just as there's a built-in cognitive faculty that forms belief in God (to the extent that it is repaired), there is much to be said for the existence of a *moral* cognitive faculty. In Paul's letter to the Romans, just after explaining that all humans—believer and unbeliever alike—see something of God in nature, he tells us that every human comes equipped with a sense of right and wrong.

> Indeed, when Gentiles, who do not have the law, do by nature things required by the law, they are a law for themselves, even though they do not have the law, since they show that the requirements of the law are written on their hearts, their consciences also bearing witness, and their thoughts now accusing, now even defending them.[6]

This moral cognitive faculty, like the *sensus divinitatis*, has been damaged by sin and therefore needs repair and guidance. Even so, it produces some of our strongest beliefs. There are very few things we're more certain of than our moral judgments. Suppose you encountered someone who argued that Hitler's actions during World War II weren't wrong. You would, I imagine, reject the argument outright—regardless of how sophisticated and subtle the argument was—simply because it gave the wrong answer. Your belief that the conclusion is false would be far stronger than your belief in any of the argument's premises.

Again, when the Bible alludes to our moral cognitive faculty, it isn't suggesting that there are moral *arguments* that humans will find compelling. It's not that there aren't such arguments; rather the Bible just doesn't have arguments or inferences in mind here at all. Nevertheless, just as in the case of arguments related to creation, arguments related to morality figure prominently in debates over God's existence.

So, I'll focus on arguments that are important because of the way humans are made, because of the kind of creatures humans *are*. And what you think humans are—and what you think they're *for*—will vary depending on which side of the debate you stand.

Perspective is everything.

FOR YOUR ARSENAL

- Two of the most important and powerful objections to belief in God are (1) science shows that God doesn't exist and (2) suffering and evil show that God doesn't exist.

- We can see why these two potential defeaters are so prominent. Each corresponds to an important cognitive faculty: the first to our *sensus divinitatis*, our ability to see God in creation; the second to our moral cognitive faculty, our ability to see good and evil, right and wrong.

PART 2

"Science Has Shown There's No God"

11

GALILEO AND THE
NEEDLESS WAR

US VERSUS THEM?

In an interview with *ABC News's* Diane Sawyer, physicist Stephen Hawking, the most respected scientist since Einstein, said, "There is a fundamental difference between religion, which is based on authority, [and] science, which is based on observation and reason." In the end, he continued, "Science will win because it works."[1]

Why think that there's a battle between science and religion, or even a friendly competition? After all, many scientists believe in God—something like 40 percent worldwide.[2] And in the United States, that number may be as high as 90 percent.[3] Moreover, the U.S. National Academy of Sciences officially states that there's nothing for science and religion to fight over: "Science is a way of knowing about the natural world. It is limited to explaining the natural world through natural causes. Science can say nothing about the supernatural. Whether God exists or not is a question about which science is neutral."[4]

The late Stephen Jay Gould, a Harvard paleontologist, agreed. Despite his ardent atheism, he just as ardently believed that science and religion have nothing to say to one another, that they each have their own, hermetically sealed domains or "magisteria."

> To say it for my colleagues and for the umpteenth millionth time (from college bull sessions to learned treatises): science simply cannot (by its legitimate methods) adjudicate the issue of God's possible superintendence of nature. We neither affirm nor deny it; we simply can't comment on it as scientists.[5]

Gould captured this important idea in the acronym "NOMA": non-overlapping magisteria.

Not everyone is happy with this sort of neutrality. Victor Stenger—in a chapter titled "The Sword of Science"—says that the declared truce is really just a pragmatic move, "to avoid conflict with the majority of ordinary citizens who are believers."[6] According to Stenger, it seems, Gould and the Academy are chicken. And Richard Dawkins asks, "Despite the confident, almost bullying, tone of Gould's assertion, what, actually, is the justification for it? Why shouldn't we comment on God as scientists?"[7] And, on the religious side, some Christians have thought that Gould marginalized their concerns and that NOMA was "tantamount to offering believers 'terms of surrender.'"[8]

Nevertheless, some people are trying to make nice. Of course, genuine peacemaking is predicated on genuine conflict. There's a war, say the peacemakers, but it's an unnecessary one.

And they're right.

THE POWER OF ADVERTISING

The war between science and religion is largely a concocted one. In the nineteenth century, the "warfare view" of science and religion had some excellent public relations. Two American secularists wrote revisionist histories that became extremely popular, especially among a small, vocal group of antireligious scientists. The "terms of the debate" between science and religion were set by Andrew Dickson White's *A History of the Warfare of Science with Theology in Christendom* (1896) and John William Draper's *History of the Conflict between Science and Religion* (1874).[9] The ghosts of these books still haunt our academic halls. Victor Stenger, for example, approvingly cites these books to prove that there's an inherent conflict between science and religion, despite "many attempts to minimize and even eliminate the claimed conflict."[10]

And though these early shots came from the United States, English scientists—like Thomas Henry Huxley (called Darwin's bulldog "for his aggressive advocacy of evolution")—gave their "enthusiastic support for this revisionist history."[11] The goal of these men, says historian Frank M. Turner, was "to expand the influence of scientific ideas for the purpose of secularizing society rather than for the goal of advancing science internally. Secularization was their goal; science, their weapon."[12]

This is the secularist's strategy. But what exactly is their story?

IN THE BEGINNING

Their claim is that religion has opposed science from the beginning—and vice versa. The conflict, they say, is unavoidable, as evidenced by Galileo's trouble with the Roman Catholic Church in the early 1600s.

In 1616, nearly seventy-five years after Copernicus, the Catholic Church condemned "Copernicanism"—the view that the earth moves around a stationary sun—and put Copernicus's work on the *Index of Prohibited Books*. The church's official position—although not held by everyone in the church—was that Scripture clearly taught that the sun moved around a stationary earth. After all, it was argued, the Bible explicitly says that God miraculously made the sun stand still, implying that the sun must have been moving to begin with (see Joshua 10).

Some years after Copernicus finally made this list of dubious distinction—in 1633—the Inquisition in Rome found the Italian scientist Galileo Galilei guilty of "vehement suspicion of heresy" for his adherence to Copernicanism (a less serious verdict than "proven guilty of heresy"). As part of Galileo's sentence, the Inquisition forced him to recant his view that the earth moves, and he spent the rest of his life under house arrest, dying alone in his villa, entirely blind.

This David-and-Goliath story is a stirring one. And what more does a cause need than a sympathetic martyr? Here we have a rational scientist who valiantly stands alone, defiant against the ignorant and cruelly authoritative religious fanatics. Who would *you* root for?

Despite making for better operas, novels, and plays, this Galileo is largely a work of fiction, a mythical creature of fancy.

AMONG CHRISTIANS; ABOUT INTERPRETATION

Galileo himself never saw his conflict as one between science and religion. For him, it was a debate among Christians. Neither was the concern merely theological. In fact, when the Inquisition first turned its attention to Copernicanism, it was in response to a priest who complained that the "Galileists," although "good Christians," "trample underfoot all of Aristotle's philosophy, which is so useful for scholastic theology."[13] Scholasticism was an amalgamation of Aristotelianism and Christianity, with its distinctions long forgotten. The church had, after a bumpy start, embraced Aristotelian "philosophy," which included Aristotle's science. The merger between Aristotelianism and Christianity made any attack on Aristotle—which is what Galileo saw himself as doing—an attack on Christianity. Scientific theories come and go, and woe to those who try to wed transitory physical theories with perennial faith.

The disagreement over Copernicanism was primarily between two scientific factions within the Christian community. And it was a disagreement over the interpretation of *texts*. The English philosopher

Francis Bacon had written that God gave humans two books. One of the books, of course, is Scripture; the other is the book of nature. On this, everyone agreed. Thomas Dixon writes,

> On all sides of the Galileo case there was agreement that it was proper and rational both to seek accurate knowledge of the world through observations of nature and also to base one's beliefs on the Bible. The conflict was not between empirical science and authoritarian religion but rather between differing views within the Catholic Church about how to interpret nature and Scripture, especially when they seemed to disagree.[14]

In this case, one text seemed to be telling us that the earth moved, the other that the sun did. But since God had written both books, we must be interpreting one of them incorrectly. But which?

Galileo was clear that "the Holy Scripture can never lie or err, and that its declarations are absolutely and inviolably true."[15] But, he conceded, "some of its interpreters and expositors can sometimes err in various ways."[16] So maybe, said Galileo, the problem is the *interpretation* of Scripture. Although it seems that Scripture says that the sun moves, perhaps it's merely speaking of the way things appear to us.

Or another possibility, said Galileo, is that the Bible really *is* saying that the sun moves, but God is just accommodating himself to the beliefs of the ancient Israelites. They would have presumably been distracted from the real point of the story—that God miraculously lengthened the day—by the shocking announcement that the earth moves, not the sun. And, continued Galileo, the point of Scripture isn't to tell us about science. He said,

> the authority of the Holy Writ has merely the aim of persuading men of those articles and propositions which are necessary for their salvation and surpass all human reason, and so could not become credible through some other science or any other means except the mouth of the Holy Spirit itself.[17]

And although this sounds quite modern, the "accommodation" view was common in Galileo's day.

Of course there was a third text that figured heavily in the debate: Aristotle's impressive canon. Aristotle and Scripture seemed to agree that the earth held pride of place in the universe, located at the center. Moreover, this view was such an integral part of Aristotle's philosophy that, if denied, much of Aristotle's science would have to go. And that was something the scientific establishment—being Aristotelian—would simply not tolerate.

DENYING OUR SENSES

But if the earth did move around the sun, we'd not only have to change our interpretation of Scripture and discard valuable Aristotelian doctrines, we'd also have to deny the apparent testimony of our senses. There are very few things more apparent to our senses than that the earth is stationary. We don't feel it move, see it move, hear it move, smell it move, or taste it move. And Galileo clearly recognized this.

> Nor can I ever sufficiently admire the outstanding acumen of those who have taken hold of this opinion [Copernicanism] and accepted it as true; they have through sheer force of intellect done such violence to their own senses as to prefer what reason told them over that which sensible experience plainly showed them to the contrary. For the arguments against the whirling of the earth which we have already examined are very plausible, as we have seen; and the fact that the Ptolemaics and Aristotelians and all their disciples took them to be conclusive is indeed a strong argument of their effectiveness.[18]

This is one of the most unexpected and ironic passages in the history of science. Galileo—the man responsible for making observation and experiment a central part of science—said that denying our senses can be a virtue; seeing isn't necessarily believing. He cheerfully declared that the lack of observational evidence for a moving earth makes believing it all the more admirable.[19]

Of course, we're not really denying our senses when we believe that the earth moves, only their natural interpretation. On both sides, everyone would agree that *there's* the sun, for example. Recall Wittgenstein's remark that this is exactly what it would look like if the earth moved; after all, it does. What our senses tell us is ambiguous.

DON'T BE TOO HASTY

Galileo's main worry—aside from the scientific concern of determining whether the sun really does move—was that, if the church were to make a rash and mistaken judgment on the issue, it could seriously damage its witness to the unbelieving world. In his famous *Letter to the Grand Duchess Christina*, Galileo appealed—as he would frequently throughout the letter—to the authority of the exalted church father Augustine of Hippo. Galileo believed that Augustine was right when the ancient saint said,

> The distressing thing is not so much that an erring man [i.e., the believer] should be laughed at, but that our authors [of Scripture] should be thought by outsiders to believe such things, and should be criticized and rejected as ignorant, to the great detriment of those whose salvation we care about. For how can they believe our books in regard to the resurrection of the dead, the hope of eternal life, and the kingdom of heaven, when they catch a Christian committing an error about something they know very well, when they declare false his opinion taken from those books, and when they find these full of fallacies in regard to things they have already been able to observe or to establish by unquestionable argument?[20]

Galileo tried to make clear that he merely wanted the church authorities to take the time to carefully weigh the evidence on such an important issue: "I propose not that [Copernicus's] book should not be condemned, but that it should not be condemned without understanding, examining, or even seeing it."[21] Of course, Galileo believed that upon careful consideration, the church would see that the evidence weighs in favor of Copernicanism. But the church hurriedly decided that the evidence wasn't in favor of Copernicanism.

To be fair, however, even on purely scientific grounds, Galileo didn't have the requisite evidence—at least by the standards of his time. And even the Catholic Church's most eminent theologian—Cardinal Robert Bellarmine—entertained the possibility that someday scientists might demonstrate the truth of Copernicanism. If they did, he agreed that the church would have to modify "with great care" our understanding of the relevant biblical passages. But, he continued, "I will not believe that there is such a demonstration, until it is shown to me."[22]

Unfortunately, of the handful of men who decided to condemn Copernicus, none were scientists or mathematicians. This is less than ideal. It's difficult to competently evaluate or judge the scientific and mathematical evidence without competence in either.[23] Even though it turned out that these men were correct in judging that Galileo lacked the requisite scientific evidence (even according to his own standards), it's questionable whether they judged so for the right reasons. There are times when a scientific theory *can* be judged by an intelligent layman ("you don't have to be a weatherman to know which way the wind blows"), but this was not one of those times.

In any case, the church hastily spoke out on Copernicanism, just as Galileo had feared. Copernicanism was officially condemned and the Catholic Church prohibited anyone from teaching it. Disappointed, Galileo turned to other things.

"PERMISSION TO SPEAK FREELY, SIR"

But things began looking up when Galileo's longtime friend and admirer Maffeo Barberini became Pope Urban VIII. In fact, years before, Barberini had written an ode praising Galileo's scientific discoveries and marveling at the new world they revealed. This was the opportunity Galileo was looking for. Perhaps Copernicus could now be removed from the *Index*.

Galileo obtained the pope's permission to write about the Copernican theory—but only as a purely theoretical hypothesis, not as the literal truth. The goal was to show the rest of the world that the Catholic Church—and Italy—wasn't rejecting Copernicanism because of scientific ignorance.

It took more than five years for Galileo to complete his *Dialogue Concerning the Two Chief World Systems*, largely due to recurring bouts of his lifelong illness. And, although the church approved the work, a series of tragic misunderstandings resulted in things going about as badly as they could have.

For one thing, the pope felt that Galileo had made fun of him in the dialogue, casting him as the hapless Aristotelian. Also, Galileo made Copernicanism look like more than a theoretical mathematical tool—he made Copernicanism look *too* good.

To make matters worse, the pope believed that Galileo had deceived him when initially asking for permission to write on Copernicanism. While the book was being approved, an unsigned notary document from 1616 mysteriously appeared, saying the Catholic Church told Galileo that he was to never even talk about Copernicanism, much less support it. Why, asked the pope, had Galileo hidden this important piece of information? Urban was furious. And he was hurt—his friend had betrayed him.

Galileo had never seen the document.

The pope's fury led to Galileo's condemnation. Biographer James Reston writes that "one remark by Pope Urban VIII explains the entire Galileo affair: 'He did not fear to make sport of me.'"[24]

MYTH BUSTING

Stephen Hawking and Leonard Mlodinow retell the legend that after Galileo recanted before the Inquisition, he "is said to have muttered under his breath '*Eppur si muove*,' 'But still it moves.'"[25] This is a compelling image of the defiant individualist we've come to admire. Unfortunately, say scholars, there is no evidence for it, a mere fable cherished by those who wistfully recount it.[26]

In fact, near the end of his life, while under house arrest, Galileo actually counted his loyalty to the church as one of his greatest consolations. In a private letter to a friend, when he was no longer in any danger, Galileo wrote,

> This afflicts me less than people may think possible, for I have two sources of perpetual comfort—first, that in my writings there cannot be found the faintest shadow of irreverence towards the Holy Church; and second, the testimony of my own conscience, which only I and God in Heaven thoroughly know. And He knows that in this cause for which I suffer, though many might have spoken with more learning, none, not even the ancient Fathers, have spoken with more piety or with greater zeal for the Church than I.[27]

Moreover, the "cause" that Galileo mentioned isn't *science*. Rather, according to Stillman Drake—the twentieth-century's premier Galileo scholar—"the cause for which Galileo suffered, in his own view, was clearly not Copernicanism but sound theology and Christian zeal."[28]

The Scientific Revolution of the 1600s—of which the Copernican revolution was a part—was just that, a revolution, an overturning of an old scientific system (Aristotelianism). It was science against science. And throughout, the scientists were Christian. Galileo saw himself as a new kind of Christian scientist, one who eschewed rigid appeal to pagan philosophers (such as Aristotle). Later in the century, Isaac Newton, Robert Boyle, and others involved in England's Royal Society, would see themselves similarly. These scientists—often called "virtuosi"—believed that science is a natural outworking of a Christian desire to know God and his creation.[29]

DAMAGE CONTROL

The warfare view of science and religion has seeped into the soil of Western civilization, poisoning our water. It doesn't matter that modern research has shown, for example, that the scientists involved in the development of modern science during the 1600s were Christians. Never mind that Newton, the culmination of the Scientific Revolution, was a devout Christian who wrote far more on theology than all other subjects combined. The cleanup is going to take a long time.

And there will be continued resistance to the cleanup. The Christian nature of early modern science isn't pleasant news for those who wish to keep religion and science at each other's throats. And whenever the facts of the Christian origin of modern science become difficult to ignore, atheists look for an alternative explanation for this inconvenient truth. Richard Dawkins spins things this way:

> Newton did indeed claim to be religious. So did almost everybody until—significantly I think—the nineteenth century, when there was less social and judicial pressure than in earlier centuries to profess religion, and more scientific support for abandoning it.[30]

Stenger, although he concedes that Galileo, Newton, "and many other great scientists have been believers," claims that "anyone living at that time didn't have much choice."[31] Bertrand Russell said something similar: "The immense majority of intellectually eminent men disbelieve in Christian religion, but they conceal the fact in public, because they are afraid of losing their incomes."[32] Apparently, scientists like Galileo, Boyle, and Newton were merely pretending to be Christians.

Given the unvarnished silliness of these attempts, other atheists think it would be better to ridicule the early scientists as an unwashed, ignorant lot. Christopher Hitchens said that "Sir Isaac Newton was prey to the most idiotic opinions about alchemy."[33] And of course, if Newton held beliefs as wacky as those, his Christianity is guilty by association. Again, never mind that alchemy was the chemistry of the time, and that Newton was influenced in his alchemy by the father of chemistry, Robert Boyle. That's just historical pedantry.

To the minds of the fathers of modern science, their work was a natural way of reveling in God's creation, and glorifying God by studying his works. And atheists might concede all this. Even if it was rational to believe in God at one time, science, we are told, has since shown that there is no God—or at least it certainly hasn't uncovered any evidence in his favor. In any case, there's no longer any room for God. Nor do we need him; he doesn't do anything anyway.

FOR YOUR ARSENAL

- The alleged conflict between science and religion began in earnest with two nineteenth-century revisionist histories of the relation between Christianity and science.

- Galileo's trial is incorrectly seen as the origin of an inherent conflict between religion and a secular science. The "Galileo affair," however, was a conflict between *Christians* and about how best to interpret two texts: Scripture and the book of nature.

- Galileo remained a devout Catholic his entire life. His condemnation by the Catholic Church resulted primarily from personal conflicts with the Jesuits and Pope Urban VIII.

12

THE LAZY GOD

LAPLACE DON'T NEED NO GOD

Christopher Hitchens identified precisely when God became superfluous.[1] The auspicious moment occurred a century after Newton, when Napoleon Bonaparte met with Pierre-Simon Laplace, the French mathematician and physicist. Laplace presented the emperor with a copy of his monumental *Celestial Mechanics*, a work in which he spread Newton's physics further through the solar system.[2] It had taken twenty-six years for Laplace to complete this enormous five-volume work. As Napoleon received it, he remarked to his honored guest, "Monsieur Laplace, they tell me you have written this large book on the system of the universe and have never even mentioned its Creator." Laplace coolly replied, "I have no need of this hypothesis."[3] "*And*," wrote Hitchens, "*neither do we*."[4]

Many of us are unaware that Laplace's book rendered God unnecessary. But now that we've heard, it would also be nice to know just exactly what it is we no longer need God for. Moreover, we may also wonder whether science can even show such a thing.

It's best to wade into this issue from the shallow end, with Laplace's notion of a hypothesis. After all, it was as a hypothesis that Laplace no longer needed God. And unless we understand what a hypothesis is, we can't say—not with a straight face—that we know the kinds of things science can and cannot do.

THE REAL QUESTION IS "WHY?"

We usually think of a hypothesis as a tentative idea, with emphasis on the *tentative*. People say, for example, "Evolution is a hypothesis, not a fact." Although a hypothesis is tentative, uncertainty isn't what's central to the notion. Rather, a hypothesis is a *potential explanation*. Evolution is a hypothesis insofar as it explains what we observe in nature: the fossil record, functions of organs, or whatever. Evolution is one answer to "Why do things look *this* way?" or "Why does the fossil record have these peculiar characteristics?" or "How did the zebra get its stripes?"

And the things over which scientists fight are usually explanations, not the observations themselves. Everyone agrees that the sun is located at such and such a location—it's *there* in the morning and over *there* in the evening. The thornier questions concern *why* things are the way they are or *how* they got that way, what *caused* them to be like that. An explanation—and therefore a hypothesis—is an answer to a "why" or "how" question. *Why* is the sun over there in the morning and over there in the evening? Is it because it's actually moving or because the earth is rotating?

But the inherent uncertainty of a hypothesis *is* important. Uncertainty *per se* isn't the issue—after all, very few of our beliefs enjoy absolute certainty. Rather, it's that hypotheses aren't as certain as *observations*. We don't directly observe hypotheses; we reason to them. And this isn't surprising: the most common form of reasoning in science, you'll recall, is "inference to the best *explanation*." This is how scientists arrive at hypotheses—at scientific theories. And, obviously enough, it's by inference, not by direct observation.

Centuries ago, when wondering why there are darker areas on the moon, scientists (or natural philosophers, as they were still called) supposed that these were optical effects of the earth's atmosphere. At least that was one hypothesis, a possible explanation. We didn't actually "see" that these dark areas were caused by the earth's atmosphere. But once Galileo finally saw (through his "spy glass") that these darker areas are really blemishes on the moon itself, we knew that the atmospheric hypothesis was wrong. We had a new explanation—surface blemishes. (This was alarming because we thought the moon was made of a perfect, unchanging celestial substance called aether.) And because Galileo observed these blemishes, this new explanation could not be called a hypothesis, despite explaining why there appear to be dark areas on the moon.

All hypotheses are explanations, but not all explanations are hypotheses. Hypotheses are inferred explanations, not observed explanations.

But nonscientists—ordinary humans like you and me—also ask "why" questions, arriving at hypotheses of our own. Suppose I see that the gate to my backyard is open. It's normally closed and so I'd like to know *why* it's open—what caused it to open.[5] There are any number of possibilities, some more plausible than others. One likely scenario is that one of my children left the gate open (they've done it before). Or maybe *I* forgot to close it. Another possibility is that a stranger left it open after rummaging through my shed. That's less likely, but likely enough. Any of these scenarios is a potential explanation for the open gate, and therefore a hypothesis.

THE GOD HYPOTHESIS

When Laplace told Napoleon that he didn't need God as a hypothesis, he meant that he didn't need God as an explanation. But an explanation for what? Presumably, as an explanation for whatever he was considering in his magnificent book. And, among other things, his book contained facts about the heavens, mathematical descriptions of the planets' motions, descriptions arrived at using Newton's physics.

But Newton hadn't been able to describe planetary motions exactly; he was left with small deviations suggesting that the universe is unstable, that the planets wouldn't remain in their orbits without periodic adjustment. Yet it was clear that they did stay in their orbits. It just wasn't clear why.

According to Newton, the planets stayed put because God periodically corrected their motions. But Newton immediately caught flak. His nemesis, German philosopher and mathematician Gottfried Leibniz, complained that Newton's God was an incompetent craftsman: "God Almighty," teased Leibniz, "wants to wind up his watch from time to time: otherwise it would cease to move. He had not, it seems, sufficient foresight to make it a perpetual motion [machine]."[6]

A century later, however, Laplace had improved the accuracy of the mathematical descriptions, discovering that the solar system isn't unstable after all. Rather, its motion is merely periodic like a swing, undulating back and forth. Laplace, therefore, didn't need God's intervention to account for the cosmological upkeep.

Laplace, however, probably didn't mean that he didn't need God for anything whatsoever. Even less did he mean—at least his comments themselves didn't imply—that God doesn't exist. Why then would atheists like Hitchens refer to Laplace's remark as a sign that we had grown out of our immature belief in God, as "one puts 'away childish things'?"[7] Wouldn't Laplace's findings merely be evidence that God made a universe that's more orderly than we thought?

THE GOD OF THE GAPS

Newton had needed a hypothesis for why the planets didn't eventually wander off into space or plummet into the sun.[8] And so—just as there is *whenever* we want an explanation—there was a gap in Newton's understanding. Newton filled this gap with God, in particular, with God's regular intervention. And there has been no end of the trouble since.

Newton's use of God as scientific caulk is why atheists now take pleasure in Laplace's meeting with Napoleon. Laplace's dismissal is, in miniature, what science has allegedly done in general over the last few centuries. Whenever believers refer to God as the cause of an event in nature, atheists now derisively refer to it as a God-of-the-gaps explanation. And the problem with a God-of-the-gaps explanation is that sometimes we can fill a previously God-filled gap with a *natural* explanation. In these cases we discover that God is an artificial filler. And as we replace ever more supernatural explanations with natural ones, it can give the distinct impression that we have fewer and fewer reasons to believe in God. "Creationists," Dawkins says, "eagerly seek a gap in present-day knowledge or understanding. If an apparent gap is found, it is *assumed* that God, by default, must fill it. What worries thoughtful theologians . . . is that gaps shrink as science advances."[9] Science, says Sam Harris, is a juggernaut: "Religion once offered answers to many questions that have now been ceded to the care of science. This process of scientific conquest and religious forfeiture has been relentless, one directional, and utterly predictable."[10]

Atheists have extrapolated this past shrinkage, and are now wholly optimistic, expecting that all possible explanations will be purely natural. Science, according to them, will march right over God. No more God of the gaps, and so no more God. Laplace's response to Napoleon is seen as a promissory note, partial fulfillment of a long-awaited prophecy.

And so we come to one of the main general arguments against God's existence: science has shown that he is simply not needed to explain the physical world. Because of God's past performance, he has been laid off from his explanatory job. Dawkins enjoys the idea of an unemployed God, referring to a book in which Peter Atkins postulates a hypothetical lazy God who tries to get away with as little as possible in order to make a universe containing life. Atkins's lazy God is [a] *dues otiosus*—literally God at leisure, unoccupied, unemployed, superfluous, useless. Step by step, Atkins succeeds in reducing the amount of work the lazy God has to do until he finally ends up doing nothing at all: he might as well not bother to exist. My memory vividly hears Woody Allen's perceptive whine: "If it turns out that there is a God, I don't think that he's evil. But the worst you can say about him is that basically he's an underachiever."[11]

Hitchens, too, announced that there is no more explanatory work for God: "Religion has run out of justifications. Thanks to the telescope and the microscope, it no longer offers an explanation of anything important."[12] No doubt you are disappointed to hear this.

AN INTERVENTION

Of course, there's something right about the atheist's complaint of God-of-the-gaps theology. We can, as believers, agree that such a God isn't all that great, nor even much good. He's certainly not a God that a Christian should take seriously. The problem with the God of the gaps isn't that there are dwindling gaps into which we can fit him; rather, the problem is that the God of the gaps is a feeble and pathetic God to begin with. Although he created the universe, he takes a largely laissez-faire approach to the cosmos, allowing it to run almost entirely on its own.[13] *Almost* entirely. He saves a few operations for himself; he sometimes overrides the laws of nature—perhaps raising someone from the dead or parting some water here and there.

This God has been familiar since the Enlightenment at least. But Plantinga identifies some important differences between

God and the God of the gaps. God, according to traditional Christianity, is constantly and directly involved in creation. He is, at this very moment, keeping the cosmos in existence and actively governing all its aspects.[14] God didn't simply wind up the universe, letting it largely run by itself. The universe isn't like that. Instead, nothing would continue to exist—the universe, the angels, you—if God did not continually sustain it. Nor would anything in the universe *do* anything without his causing it, either directly or indirectly.

And this has important implications for an extremely popular argument against miracles. Hume famously defined miracles as "a violation of a law of nature." Echoing this, Dawkins says, "I suspect that alleged miracles provide the strongest reason many believers have for their faith; and miracles, by definition, violate the principles of science."[15] Therefore, because laws of nature are supposedly inviolable—that's what it means to be a law of nature after all—miracles are, by definition, impossible. Miracles would be like married bachelors and square circles—impossible.

But laws of nature aren't *objects* out there, inviolably causing things to happen. Rather, they're descriptions of the way nature ordinarily behaves, statements of regularities. And so according to Christian theism, laws are descriptions of the way *God* ordinarily does things. Miracles aren't events in which God finally shows up to violate some law; miracles are simply instances when God does things differently. "Indeed," as Plantinga says,

> the whole *interventionist* terminology—speaking of God as *intervening* in nature, or *intruding* into it, or *interfering* with it, or *violating* natural law—all this goes with God-of-the-gaps theology, not with serious theism. According to [serious theism], God is already and always intimately acting in nature, which depends from moment to moment for its existence upon immediate divine activity; there isn't and couldn't be any such thing as his "'intervening'" in nature.[16]

God doesn't intervene—he's constantly active in the universe, controlling it and keeping it in existence. Were he to cease his continual activity for even a moment, all matter, space, time, and whatever else the universe is made of, would vanish into nothingness.

GOD IS NOT A SOLUTION TO YOUR PROBLEM

But, Plantinga points out, there's another problem with a God-of-the-gaps theology. The God-of-the-gaps proponent thinks of the God-filled gaps *as reasons for believing in God.* To be sure, explanations referring to God's activity—we'll see some legitimate ones later—would be evidence for God's existence. But it would be a colossal mistake to think of these as the Christian's reason for believing in God. We saw earlier that Christians don't ordinarily base their belief in God on any inference whatsoever, much less on inferences from explanatory gaps to God's existence. Rather, Christians typically believe by way of a properly functioning cognitive faculty—what we called the *sensus divinitatis*—and the work of the Holy Spirit.

Notice, then, that Christians don't postulate a God *in order to* explain some physical phenomenon.[17] That is, they don't first decide that God is a really good explanation for some event and then—because God is a good explanation—go on to believe in God. For the Christian, God is obviously an imminently reasonable explanation of many things; but ordinarily it isn't *because* God is a good explanation that Christians believe in God. As we've said, Christians rarely believe in God by way of inference or argument.

Of course, believers will think that God spectacularly explains things we see in nature. And this will no doubt strengthen their belief in God, as it should. In fact, one of the goals of this book is to do just that. But as we've seen, there's a difference between instituting a belief and strengthening it.

FOR YOUR ARSENAL

- *Explanation*: an answer to a why question.

- *Hypothesis*: a potential explanation of some fact we already believe. We infer, rather than observe, hypotheses.

- A God-of-the-gaps explanation is one in which God's activity is used to explain physical phenomena when no natural explanation is forthcoming. When a natural explanation is eventually found, thereby removing the explanatory need for God, people often conclude that there's one less reason to believe in God.

- Although it's possible that God will legitimately figure in explanations of physical phenomena, these explanations are not typically used by Christians as reasons to initially believe in God. They can, however, strengthen or support belief in God.

- God does not merely intervene in creation, but continually sustains and governs it. He is not merely a God of the gaps.

13

THERE'S NO NEED TO EXPLAIN

IT SURE *LOOKS* DESIGNED

Remember the potential defeater we're addressing in this section: *science has shown that there's no God.* Now some people puzzle over this claim, wondering how on earth anyone came to believe it. Hasn't science, after all, strongly encouraged our suspicion that nature is the product of great genius and cunning? The universe seems to be "a put up job," as David Berlinski calls it.[1] Philosopher Neil Manson writes,

> A series of breakthroughs in physics and observational astronomy led to the development of the Big Bang model and the discovery that the Universe is highly structured, with precisely defined parameters such as age, mass, entropy (degree of disorder), curvature, temperature, density, and rate of expansion. Using clever experimentation and astounding instrumentation,

physical cosmologists were able to determine the values of these parameters to remarkably precise degrees. The specificity of the Universe prompted theoretical exploration of how the Universe would have been if the values of its parameters had been different. This led to the discovery of numerous "anthropic coincidences" and supported the claim that the Universe is fine-tuned for life—that is, that the values of its parameters are such that, if they differed even slightly, life of any sort could not possibly have arisen in the Universe.[2]

Even atheists agree on this much. Richard Dawkins, for example, concedes that parameters such as these are in their respective "Goldilocks zone"—they're just right.[3]

We can put things this way: nearly everyone agrees that the universe *appears* to have been designed, and with exquisite care. Surely this requires an explanation. And what better explanation for this uncanny appearance of design than that it *was* designed?

So what's the problem?

WELL, DUH

While nearly everyone may agree on the *appearances*, the real debates, as we saw, are usually over *explanations*. And there's a very different explanation of the universe's delicate just-so structure, one that doesn't refer to a designer. "Look," this alternative explanation goes, "if the universe *weren't* just so, we wouldn't be around to consider it being just so. What else would you expect, and therefore what's there to explain?" This response is based on the *anthropic principle*, which says, according to Dawkins, "that we could only be discussing the question in the kind of universe that was capable of producing us."[4]

And the anthropic principle could not be more true. In fact, that's its only virtue. As an explanation of the universe's people-friendly appearance, it's a miserable failure. After all, it's little more than a restatement of the very thing we're trying to explain: that the universe is just right for life. We know *that*. What we don't understand is *why*. "Why," asks Dawkins himself, "did it have to be the kind of universe which seems almost as if, in the words of the theoretical physicist Freeman Dyson, it 'must have known we were coming'?"[5] The anthropic principle doesn't say. And that's because it doesn't even try.

Philosopher Peter van Inwagen calls the invocation of the anthropic principle "one of the most annoyingly obtuse arguments in the history of philosophy." He considers an analogy:

> Suppose you are in a situation in which you must draw a straw from a bundle of 1,048,576 straws of different lengths, and suppose it has been decreed that if you don't draw the shortest straw in the bundle you will be instantly and painlessly killed: you will be killed so fast you won't have time to realize you didn't draw the shortest straw. Reluctantly—but you have no alternative— you draw a straw and are astonished to find yourself alive and holding the shortest straw. What should you conclude?[6]

You should probably conclude, according to van Inwagen, that someone has set up the situation so that you would be guaranteed to choose the shortest straw. And if I asked you to explain why you happened to pick the shortest straw, you wouldn't (I hope) reply, "Because if I hadn't, I wouldn't be here." If you did, my considered response would be, "Well, duh."

The question then is this: Why would anyone believe that the anthropic principle is a good explanation? The answer to this question, it seems to me, helps us see why many scientists think that science shows that God doesn't exist.

A CHANGE OF PLANS

Remember that in the seventeenth century, Galileo's troubles began when he mussed up the hair of the scientific establishment, an establishment comprised of Aristotelians. Not only did Galileo argue against the Aristotelian view that the earth moved around the sun—that was controversial enough—he also supported his position with a method just as contentious. And when the rules themselves aren't agreed upon, everything else becomes secondary. If the foundations be destroyed, what shall the righteous do?

In any case, the rules changed, and Galileo overthrew a two-thousand-year-old scientific method. Galileo's rules still rule.

One of the distinctive features of Aristotelian science was its goal. Aristotle was ultimately interested in explanations, in particular, causes of physical phenomena. Merely describing how the physical phenomena behaved wasn't enough. For example, we can *see* that heavy objects fall; that much is obvious. The real question, according to Aristotle, is why they fall, what causes them to fall.

In the case of falling objects, Aristotle began by pointing out that all terrestrial objects—all objects below the heavens—are composed of four elements: earth, air, fire, and water. Each of these four elements has its own inherent *nature* that makes it behave uniquely, its own personality. The earthy element's nature, for example, causes earthy things to move toward the center of the universe. And so, for Aristotelians, earthy objects moved toward the center of the earth. (People had long realized that the earth is round.) The center of the universe is the earthy element's natural place of rest, the place to which the element's nature directs it. This internal nature, then, said the Aristotelians, is what causes heavy objects to fall. Natures—mysterious though they may be—were what explained why objects fall.

Galileo was extremely skeptical of this notion of natures. Are there really such things? Maybe, maybe not. It's difficult to say. In fact, said Galileo, it's *too* difficult to say. Better to leave those questions—the fundamental causes of falling, for example—for when we actually have decent methods for answering them. Galileo believed that science should stick to what it can actually do, which is mostly just describe. And ideally, these descriptions should be couched in mathematical language. All this is difficult enough without chasing explanations.

At the time, most other scientists believed that this was a downgrading of the scientific endeavor, making science a discipline for mere technicians and recipe followers, not for natural philosophers (i.e., genuine scientists).

Decades after Galileo, the demotion of science incited resistance to Newton's marvelous mathematical theories. Describing how objects behave under the influence of gravity was fine, but it wasn't genuine science. And the centerpiece of Newton's work—his law of universal gravitation—is "merely" a mathematical equation that states the way in which two objects attract one another. It never explains why they are attracted. To be sure, their attractiveness is due to gravity, but "gravity" is just another word for "whatever causes attractiveness." Newton was clear that we don't know what gravity *is*. And so he made a point to omit gravity's fundamental nature from his official theory. He famously said regarding gravity, "I feign no hypotheses." It means, "I'm not going to just make something up."

Newton's refusal to provide a hypothesis or explanation of how objects behave under gravity's influence upset many of his contemporaries. Leibniz, Newton's old German foe, belittled him for reintroducing "occult" qualities back into science. Because Newton left gravity unexplained (where it remains today), he was leaving it mysterious, even spooky. Newton, his opponents believed, was returning science to benighted and superstitious times.

But like Galileo, Newton thought that identifying the cause of an object's fall simply exceeded the limits of science. Better to stay within the discipline when practicing it, Newton said. Good point.

Whatever we think of Newton's decision to limit the methods of science, he didn't for a moment believe that science exhausted all there is to say about gravity. For one thing, he believed that gravity is ultimately caused by direct divine action. But he didn't arrive at this causal explanation by way of experiment or mathematics. And so he left this explanation out of his *scientific* theory and included it in his overarching theory of the world—in his philosophy, or better, in his *theology*.

Subsequent scientists followed Newton's restricted agenda. Let's leave, they said, the question of fundamental causes to the philosophers. This is why Laplace didn't need God as a hypothesis: physics had (largely) gone out of the explanation business. At least when it came to *fundamental* explanations, explanations that themselves need no explaining.

There's nothing inherently wrong with focusing mathematical descriptions. (And outside of physics—where there are fewer mathematical descriptions—explanations are more prevalent.) But—and here's where things begin to go south—many people now call this restriction *methodological naturalism*. According to methodological naturalism, scientists may not refer to God in their scientific theories. Any description or explanation must be naturalistic.[7]

Methodological naturalism is *methodological* for the obvious reasons: it's a limitation on the method of science, on what science is allowed to do, on what it can look for. We can recognize here the U.S. National Academy of Sciences' official declaration of neutrality (and Stephen Jay Gould's NOMA—non-overlapping magisteria). Again, to specify the methods of science just makes good sense. But, says methodological naturalism, the method must be *naturalistic*—science may refer only to natural events and entities. Scientists may not explain natural phenomena with anything outside of nature—with anything *super*natural.

Of course, methodological naturalism isn't saying that there is no supernatural realm; *that's* the position of *philosophical naturalism*—plain old naturalism. The kinder, gentler methodological version just says that scientists—while wearing their scientist hats—should behave *as if* plain old naturalism is true. Scientists should pretend there's no supernatural realm. They should pretend they're atheists.

SCIENTIFIC PROVINCIALISM

We'll look more closely at the supposed virtues of methodological naturalism in the next chapter, but for now, we need to see that it encourages a deep confusion: it lulls people into believing in philosophical naturalism. Although we might say that scientists are merely following Newton in this methodological naturalism, many scientists haven't followed him far enough. They haven't emulated Newton's clear understanding that science doesn't encompass all of reality. Instead, many scientists have shrunk their notion of reality to fit science's limited reach. If it ain't science, it ain't real.

We might call this *scientific provincialism*, and it has become orthodoxy among secular scientists. Its cause, however, is a confusion of methodological naturalism with philosophical naturalism (with some wishful thinking thrown in). No wonder scientific provincialists think science has shown there's no God: by definition, there *is* nothing outside nature. It's similar to a blind person denying the existence of light.

This is why many atheists are blind to the inadequacy of the anthropic principle—it simply doesn't register that it could be inadequate. Since science has access to all of this shrunken reality, there's no need—indeed no possibility—of explaining nature's order, intelligibility, or overwhelming appearance of design. Such an explanation, after all, would have to come from outside nature. The anthropic principle's inability to explain simply mirrors science's self-imposed inability to refer to anything outside itself.

Yet science itself never claims its domain exhausts reality. Such a proclamation would be an extra-scientific claim, something that, by definition, science isn't fit to determine in the first place. It's one thing to mandate the methods of science; it is quite another to say that science is all we need to understand reality. Therefore, scientists who have made this claim have left science far behind.

And so science itself—if we limit it by methodological naturalism, turning it into what we might call naturalistic science—has never shown that there's no supernatural realm. How could it possibly do that? It has explicitly said that only the natural is within its ken, and so, by its own admission, science could never show there's no God. Furthermore, even the more meager claim that science has never found evidence for God (whether or not he exists) isn't newsworthy.

By definition, science could never do that; scientists didn't even need to bother looking. David Berlinski concludes, "If science stands opposed to religion, it is not because of anything contained in either the premises or the conclusions of the great scientific theories. They do not mention a word about God."[8]

Of course, none of this is a blemish on science; the mistake falls in the laps of scientists who—and I hate to put it this way—don't understand science. They understand how to *do* science to some degree, but they have never learned what it is they're ultimately doing, what their real goal should be. So maybe Leibniz was right: maybe Newton's restrictions on science have turned many scientists into highly skilled technicians, leaving the important questions to philosophers.

If so, methodological naturalism may not have been such a good idea. After all, who wants to leave the important questions to philosophers?

FOR YOUR ARSENAL

- Most people—believers and unbelievers alike—agree that the universe *looks* designed. The real issue is whether this is mere appearance.

- In response to the question, "Why does the universe look fine-tuned for life?" the anthropic principle answers, "If it weren't just right for life, we wouldn't be here to ask why it looks fine-tuned." This doesn't answer the question but merely states what we already knew.

- One of the reasons the anthropic principle is seen as an acceptable explanation—despite not being an explanation at all—is that modern science is interested more in descriptions than fundamental explanations. Many scientists have become accustomed to ignoring fundamental "why" questions.

- *Methodological naturalism*: the rule that God may not be referred to in science; scientists must—as scientists—act as if there is no supernatural realm.

- *Philosophical naturalism*: the view that there is no supernatural realm.

- *Scientific provincialism*: the confusion of methodological naturalism with philosophical naturalism; the view that the only reality is that which science can investigate.

- Another reason many atheists see the anthropic principle as acceptable is that atheists have confused methodological naturalism with philosophical naturalism. They have become scientific provincialists.

100% ALL NATURAL?

What if we could keep in mind that methodological naturalism is merely methodological, and so refrain from
confusing it with philosophical naturalism? Would it
then really be such a bad idea? Surely the more central methods of
science—calculating, measuring, observing—are in some sense religiously and philosophically neutral. After all, we all—believer and
unbeliever alike—see that heavy objects fall and that we need to divide
both sides of the equation by the same thing. Suppose you and I are
enjoying a bit of scientific experimenting, and we both look at a gauge
or meter whose numbers indicate something sciencey. Are we going
to disagree about where the meter points? Not usually.[1] These kinds
of considerations—whether the object falls, or whether the meter's
arrow is pointing between the 5 and 6, or whether you must divide
both sides of the equation by two—seem to be identical for everyone.

So can't we all just get along?

WHY IS SCIENCE POSSIBLE?

This suggestion is appealing. Nevertheless, the very act of doing science—of expecting to understand nature at all—depends on whether

God exists or not. Physicist Paul Davies describes some of the ways that science depends upon religious beliefs:

> It was from the intellectual ferment brought about by the merging of Greek philosophy and Judeo-Islamic-Christian thought that modern science emerged, with its unidirection linear time [rather than cyclic], its insistence on nature's rationality, and its emphasis on mathematical principles. All the early scientists such as Newton were religious in one way or another. . . . In the ensuing 300 years, the theological dimension of science has faded. People take for granted that the physical world is both ordered and intelligible. The underlying order in nature—the laws of physics—is simply accepted as given, as brute fact. Nobody asks where the laws come from—at least they don't in polite company. However, even the most atheistic scientist accepts as an act of faith [i.e., an assumption] the existence of a law-like order in nature that is at least in part comprehensible to us. So science can proceed only if the scientist adopts an essentially theological worldview.[2]

Assumptions like these have become invisible because they're familiar, and so scientists no longer appreciate the importance of these views.

Like many common assumptions, familiarity has bred contempt, or at least neglect. Victor Stenger, for example, says that science doesn't need the assumption that "nature is ordered in a rational and intelligible way." Rather, he continues, "our confidence in science is based on its practical success, not some logical deduction derived from dubious metaphysical assumptions."[3]

Stenger may be right in saying that he and other scientists trust science because it works. But his reason for trusting science is neither here nor there, except insofar as it shows that he doesn't quite grasp the nature of scientific knowledge. The real point is that the very practice of science can only be explained, or only makes sense, if nature is rational. To put it differently, the practice of science *implies* that nature is inherently rational. As Nobel Prize–winning physicist

Eugene Wigner pointed out, "[I]t is not at all natural that 'laws of nature' exist, much less that man is able to discover them."[4] Even Einstein marveled at the rationality of the universe: "The fact that it is comprehensible is a miracle."[5]

But Stenger disagrees; there's really nothing mysterious about why science works: "Science makes no assumption about the real world being 'rational.' It simply applies rational methods in taking and analyzing data, following certain rules to ensure that data are as free from error as possible, and checking the logic of our models to make sure they are self-consistent."[6] Unfortunately, merely pointing out the methods of science doesn't explain why they work. And the world—contrary to Stenger's claim—must be rational in some sense. At the very least, there must be some sort of rational "fit" between the world and our cognitive faculties. If they were wholly different from one another, there would be no reason to think that our methods would give us reliable results. Not just any old universe will allow for science. Thomas Kuhn said,

> The world . . . must also possess quite special characteristics, and we are no closer than we were at the start to knowing what these must be. That problem—What must the world be like in order that man may know it?—was not, however, created by this essay. On the contrary, it is as old as science itself, and it remains unanswered.[7]

The possibility of science—why the methods of science work—will be accounted for in different ways, depending on whether you think God exists. Methodological naturalism alone cannot account for the reliability of our scientific methods.

WHY WAS MOTHER TERESA SO NICE?

But maybe scientists like Stenger can practice science without worrying about why their practice is successful. That is, maybe they can still do science according to methodological naturalism. And so methodological naturalism may still be a fine practical rule.

But Plantinga points out ways in which our beliefs about God affect our actual scientific theories, how they affect what goes on *inside* science. There are, he says, ways in which scientists fail to follow methodological naturalism in practice. One example of Plantinga's is Herbert Simon's evolutionary answer to the "problem of altruism." Simon wonders why people like Mother Teresa do the saintly things they do. Why do they, at great costs to themselves, devote their lives to caring for others?[8]

Simon's answer is striking: people like Mother Teresa suffer from a regrettable "docility" and "bounded rationality." That is, altruistic people are gullible, believing all too readily what others tell them. They're also far too dim to realize that their altruistic behavior doesn't contribute to their fitness and survival; they fail to see that altruism just doesn't pay. Otherwise they would amend their ways and, in Plantinga's words, "get right to work on their expected number of progeny."[9]

Of course, Christians will immediately reject Simon's explanation. But the point here is that, whereas his explanation isn't very good in a Christian view of things, it is entirely respectable in an atheistic or naturalistic view of the world. That is, the plausibility of a candidate explanation—of a hypothesis—depends on our beliefs about God.

Simon's explanation assumes, for example, that humans haven't been created by God, much less created in his image. Yet this assumption isn't a product of any scientific theory—it's a *theological* add-on, a religious view. Plantinga points out that when scientists declare that humans and other organisms are merely accidents, they aren't making a scientific declaration but a philosophical or theological one (at least if we think of scientists as having to adhere to methodological naturalism). They're making inferences that follow from scientific findings *plus* theological or philosophical premises.[10] And typically one of these premises is, "God doesn't exist."

Notice therefore that not everything scientists include in their theories conforms to methodological naturalism. Science cares whether or not God exists—even if some scientists do not. God makes a difference.

WHAT WE BELIEVE DETERMINES WHAT WE BELIEVE (AGAIN)

The lesson from Simon's explanation is a general one, one we learned earlier.[11] Whenever we judge the probability of a scientific theory (or anything else), we're judging it against other things we already believe. We saw this before, but it would be difficult to overstress it. Recall the scenario where I'm trying to figure out why the gate is open. Suppose I believe my children were playing in the backyard recently. If so, I will think it extremely plausible that one of the kids left the gate open. But suppose, instead, I believe the kids are at school. Then the hypothesis that one of the kids left the gate open isn't nearly as plausible. Again, my current beliefs will significantly affect future beliefs.

Now take the standard naturalistic explanation of how humans got here: blind, unguided evolution. This explanation will be much more plausible if atheism is true than if Christianity is true. To be sure, it's not a solid theory. After all, as Plantinga says,

> Certain parts of this story . . . are, to say the least, epistemically shaky. For example, we hardly have so much as decent hints as to how life could have risen from inorganic matter just by way of the regularities known to physics and chemistry.[12]

Yet, despite the shakiness,

> Many contemporary experts and spokespersons . . . unite in declaring that evolution is no mere theory, but established fact. . . . Now why do they think so? Given the spotty character of the evidence—for example, a fossil record displaying sudden appearance and subsequent stasis and few if any genuine

examples of macroevolution, no satisfactory account of a mechanism by which the whole process could have happened, and the like—these claims of certainty seem at best wildly excessive.[13]

Perhaps this unwarranted confidence in evolution is the result of desperation. Humans—as Aristotle noted—desire to know. They especially want to know things like where humans came from and what they're here for. And evolution offers one explanation—the only explanation in sight for atheists. Because evolution has the market cornered, atheists *really* want to make this theory work.

If, on the other hand, you have other options, you'll be more likely to evaluate the evidence with a calm and sober mind.

WHY WOULD WE WANT TO PRETEND?

It seems clear then—even from just the few things we've considered—that science isn't religiously neutral. What scientists believe about God will make a difference to their science. Methodological naturalism, then, seems unrealistic for any decent sort of science.

And why would we want to be religiously neutral anyway? Methodological naturalism says, of course, that we can't refer to God in our scientific theories. But why not? Might not truths about God be useful to our scientific investigations? Why hinder science by purposefully excluding important truths? Why not use *everything* we know about the world, including the things we know about God? Why hobble ourselves with respect to the accuracy of our scientific theories? Aren't we after the truth—genuine understanding?

If a Christian psychologist, for example, uses her knowledge that humans have been created by God and have since been badly damaged by sin, wouldn't that help her understand the cause of various psychological pathologies? And more generally, knowing that the universe—and much of its contents (including you and me)—has been designed by a vast intelligence could steer scientists in their search for physical explanations, ruling out some possibilities while suggesting others. And why wouldn't these practices be a part of good science?[14] To be sure, methodological naturalism would rule them out of scientific bounds. But doesn't this just show that methodological naturalism is too restrictive, that it forces us to miss out on important truths about the world?

IS GOD A "SCIENCE STOPPER"?

But, speaking of missing out on important truths, wouldn't a rejection of methodological naturalism be a "science stopper," to use Judge John E. Jones's phrase?[15] Using God in our scientific explanations would, it seems, be a cop-out, ending the investigation when the questions become too hard. Atheists, according to Plantinga, worry that science will slow to a crawl if we explain physical phenomena by referring to God's direct activity. To answer the question, "What causes gravity?" with "God causes it" doesn't really answer the kind of questions scientists are interested in, even if such an answer is ultimately true. Scientists have more proximate concerns. Scientists want answers to questions like, "What is this made out of? What is its structure? How does it work? How is it connected with other parts of God's creation?"[16]

If we stopped science short, we'd miss out on important truths about God's creation. Christians wouldn't want that; the more we find out about creation, the more we can appreciate God and his handiwork. It seems that methodological naturalism is the perfect goad for furthering our understanding of creation. Leaving God out of science forces us to work harder, to be more inventive, more creative.

To be sure, invoking God as the direct cause of, say, the origin of life *would* be to stop science from pursuing that issue further. But even if this left nothing more for scientists to discover about life's beginnings, how would that be a strike against such an explanation? Wouldn't knowing that God didn't use secondary causes to create life but created it directly be a legitimate part of science, part of our knowledge of the universe?

The important question, then, is not whether science has its limits or stopping points, but where they are. *Any* explanation or theory is a science stopper if it satisfies our curiosity. Evolution is a science stopper in that sense. As is general relativity and quantum mechanics. Scientists are constantly looking for science stoppers in the form of true explanations. They will stop looking for an explanation once they believe they have one. We don't keep looking for our keys after we find them.

The real question, then, is whether an explanation is true, not just whether it allows scientists to call it a day.

SCIENCE CARES ABOUT GOD

So then, as Plantinga says, "It would be excessively naïve to think that contemporary science is religiously and theologically neutral."[17] He acknowledges that there may be parts of science that *are* religiously neutral, like the distance of the earth from the sun or a proof of the Pythagorean Theorem. But, he continues, other parts of science (that is, science as actually practiced, not the imaginary version rumored to obey methodological naturalism) are heavily influenced by our beliefs about God.[18]

Moreover, it often takes considerable effort to see how these beliefs affect our scientific theories. This should no longer be surprising; we saw earlier that, in general—not just in science—we're often the last ones to see how our most basic convictions affect the rest of our beliefs. We've become so used to our intellectual lenses that we see right through them.

We shouldn't be surprised, then, at the theological tint of science. Like religion, science is an effort to understand fundamental reality—including ourselves. The theory of unguided, blind evolution—what Plantinga calls the "Grand Evolutionary Myth"—is a story of origins and more:

I call this story a myth not because I do not believe it (although I do not believe it) but because it plays a certain kind of quasi-religious role in contemporary culture. It is a shared way of understanding ourselves at the deep level of religion, a deep interpretation of ourselves to ourselves, a way of telling us why we are here, where we come from, and where we are going.[19]

Science, then, despite no longer calling itself natural philosophy, still fills some of the same roles that philosophy and religion always have. At least for atheists. Unbelievers demand that science support a load far beyond its capabilities. For believers, science need not bear such a burden—it can stick to the task it was initially given.

FOR YOUR ARSENAL

- The very possibility of science depends on the order, rationality, and intelligibility of the universe. These characteristics require an intelligent designer, an intelligence that designed both the world and the human minds so that they "fit" together.

- Scientists' choices of explanations and theories often depend on whether they believe in God. Science isn't theologically neutral. That is, science doesn't actually adhere to methodological naturalism.

- One of the reasons atheists believe in unguided evolution more strongly than the evidence warrants is that they have no naturalistic alternative to evolution.

- The common charge that appealing to God as an explanation is a "science stopper" is misguided. In fact, scientists stop looking for an explanation *whenever* they believe they've found one. The real question is whether the explanation is the correct one.

15

LOOKING FOR GOD

Methodological naturalism is neither desirable nor possible—God makes a difference to the scientific endeavor. From our judgments about the plausibility of hypotheses, to the very possibility of understanding nature, our beliefs about God matter. In that sense, science isn't silent about God.

It just might be, then, that our scientific theories provide evidence for or against God's existence. And many atheists will happily agree. Of course, there will be disagreement over *what* science tells us about God. For example, Stenger's book *God: The Failed Hypothesis* is subtitled *How Science Shows That God Does Not Exist.*

In any case, it won't surprise Christians that science can show that God exists. The *sensus divinitatis* may, after all, use input from our scientific investigations to trigger faith in certain people. It wouldn't be by way of an argument, of course, but simply by seeing something of God's character in the inner workings of a cell or in the way plants turn air into food.

In fact, the best way to get someone to see God "through the things that have been made" is to get them into a position where the *sensus divinitatis* has the best chance to trigger belief in God. That is, put them in an environment in which this cognitive faculty was intended to operate: a hike in the woods or walk on the beach. Or perhaps sit them in front of one of David Attenborough's nature documentaries. Attenborough—an agnostic—shows us, with enthusiasm and eloquence, the marvels of creation, pointing out the exquisite way in which these incomprehensibly complex creatures navigate through an equally complex world. All the while, Attenborough expresses his near disbelief that these organisms are the result of blind evolution, a pure accident. The Grand Evolutionary Myth is almost too much to believe.

So we don't *need* science to tell us about God. Nevertheless, science has made many of these things even clearer, despite clamor to the contrary. Through science, we better see how delicately the universe is fit for life, its complexity and intricate structure. Whereas some people have lamented with Keats that science "unweaves the rainbow," and so removes the mystery and the cause for wonder, it seems to me it has done exactly the opposite. As Berlinski says, "There is a reason to cherish [scientific theories]. They have enlarged and not diminished our sense of the sublime."[1]

And even if the most powerful method of persuasion is a matter of *looking*, a matter of *experience*, it doesn't mean that inference or arguments can't provide solid support for our belief that God designed and created the universe and all its furniture. To be sure, believers typically aren't going to base their belief in God on such support, but support is support and we can be thankful for it.

INSTRUMENTALISM

It's safe to say, that although we can observe God's handiwork, we cannot observe *him*. This is one reason why some people think science and religion constitute entirely separate realms. Science studies what we can observe; religion—insofar as it regards God himself—obviously does not. But this characterization is wrong. For one thing—and most importantly for us here—not everything we learn from science can be observed. No one has ever observed an atom or seen the earth move. Yet it is entirely reasonable to believe in atoms and the earth's motion.

In fact, much of our story of the cosmos is *theoretical*, rather than observational. Of course, observations are crucial, just not the whole story—or even most of it. A bit of observational input often results in a torrent of theoretical output. Recall that the debate over an earth-centered and sun-centered universe wasn't primarily about the observations. People largely agreed on those. Rather the debate was over what story best explained the observations. Then, new observations began to tilt the balance of evidence in favor of Copernicanism, the sun-centered view.

Some scientists believe that the goal of science is merely to describe, predict, and control *observable* phenomena; it's not the goal of science, they say, to get at the literal truth of what goes on "behind the scenes" of observations. Some of the founders of quantum mechanics believed this about their mysterious theory. The mathematics worked and the results matched events at the observable level. But at the unobservable atomic and subatomic levels, some of the things the theory said seemed to go against the very laws of logic. But the theory worked; even if it didn't give us the sober truth about the inner workings of matter, it gave us the right answers for the world "up here." Quantum theory is, they said, a good instrument or tool for the part of the world we *can* observe.

This view is called *instrumentalism* for a good reason. It has an excellent pedigree, going all the way back to Plato and the beginnings of Western science. The mathematics with which the early Greeks described the solar system worked—it was a system of geometrical spheres—but most mathematicians didn't believe that there really are spheres causing the heavens to move. It was only later philosophers and not the mathematicians (that is, not the astronomers) who believed in literal spheres. Even the great Ptolemy said things in the *Almagest* suggesting an instrumental view of his theory.

This, of course, makes scientific theories somewhat ambivalent. Stephen Hawking says,

> Although it is not uncommon for people to say that Copernicus proved Ptolemy wrong, that is not true. . . . [We] can use either picture as a model of the universe, for our observations of the heavens can be explained by assuming either the earth or the sun to be at rest. Despite its role in philosophical debates over the nature of our universe, the real advantage of the Copernican system is simply that the equations of motion are much simpler in the frame of reference in which the sun is at rest.[2]

What matters, according to Hawking, is not whether a theory is true, but how well it works.

Still, it'd be nice to have both.

OBSERVATION VERSUS THEORY

Even though instrumentalism is more prevalent than you might think, it's still a minority view among practicing scientists. In any case, observations are usually on the judgment seat—theories must answer to our senses.

Nevertheless, observations aren't the only considerations. Because a single set of observations can be explained by more than one theory, philosophers of science say that a theory is *underdetermined* by the observational data—observations don't fully dictate which explanation is the best. There are, in fact, unlimited theories for any given set of observations. Whenever science is in the throes of theoretical change—from geocentricity to heliocentricity, from Newton's physics to Einstein's—there is a period when the theories match the world equally well.

There are, then, two main parts of science: observation and theory. When we observe events and objects in nature, we don't do so by way of an inference or argument. We just *see*. Observational beliefs are typically held in the basic way. But we *infer* theories—not only from the observational but from many things besides. Theories are the products of extremely complex arguments.

GOD: OBSERVATION OR THEORY?

So, then, just what sorts of observations should science seek when it goes looking for God? It wouldn't be reasonable to look for God himself—he is, after all, "a spirit, and doesn't have a body like men." Stenger, however, in a moment of carelessness (one hopes) says that we should be able to directly observe God:

> God is supposed to be everywhere, including inside every box. So when we search for God inside a single box, no matter how small, we should either find him, thus confirming his existence, or not find him, thus refuting his existence.[3]

Perhaps this is tongue in cheek (although the only evidence of *that* is his comment's sheer silliness). Thankfully, Stenger gains his bearings:

> If we are to hypothesize the existence of such a God, we can then infer certain observations that should be detectable, if not to the naked eye in humans, then in the careful, objective analysis of data from the highly sensitive instruments of science.[4]

The universe, according to Stenger, should somehow look different if God exists. Moreover, we should be able to predict these differences. And the Bible seems to agree: it says the heavens show the handiwork of God. Presumably, then, nature must show, in some sense, that God made it. If God hadn't, the universe wouldn't look this way—or perhaps any way at all. Stenger, therefore, appears to be right: if there's a God who is responsible for the universe, then it's reasonable to expect the universe to show it. It should have certain characteristics that science could detect. And if the universe doesn't have these characteristics—given that it should—we might have a good argument against God's existence.

CLUELESSNESS

Has science provided evidence or arguments against God's existence? Is this really even possible? And if so, can we reasonably infer from scientists' current observations and theories that there is no God?

Atheists typically tell us that the way science has shown there's no God is by failing to uncover any evidence for him. Of course, in this form, such an argument would be startlingly weak. After all, absence of evidence isn't necessarily evidence of absence. All the same, Stenger points out,

> Under some circumstances this is true, but under others it is clearly false. Absence of evidence can be strong evidence of absence when the evidence *should* be there and it is not. For example, there is absence of evidence that elephants roam Rocky Mountain National Park near where I live. Are we to conclude that elephants could still be there, in some unexplored region? Surely if elephants were there we would find some signs— droppings, crushed grass, footprints.[5]

Stenger's claim is entirely plausible. There are cases where absence of evidence can be evidence of absence. Is observational evidence for God such a case? The answer is, "It all depends." What evidence *should* be there? What kind of evidence can we reasonably expect?

Again, we shouldn't expect to find *direct* observable evidence of God himself—even with the most sensitive scientific instruments. But what about *clues* for God's existence—*indirect* observations?

What about observations for which a designer is the best explanation? Even if we can't see literal "footprints" or "crushed grass," perhaps God has left his fingerprints on the universe.

It seems that Christians could heartily acknowledge the possibility of such evidence. Perhaps we can even agree that we should *expect* these clues, not merely that they're possible. If so, and if the atheist can make a good case that there are no fingerprints of God, then it might be reasonable for some people to think that God doesn't exist.

If God exists, and if he's responsible for the existence of the universe, then we could reasonably expect to find signs of divine design. Now how would we identify and rule out such signs? That isn't easy to say, and any argument either way will be inconclusive. But there are two things to notice.

First, identifying candidates for evidence is usually easy; scientists and philosophers have never doubted that nature looks as if it were designed. The contention is over whether it merely looks this way. In any case, both sides agree that the structure of biological organisms, for example, strongly suggests that they were designed. Second, these biological candidates—and candidates in general—can be ruled out by coming up with a plausible alternative explanation, one that doesn't imply the existence of God.

So then, atheists are looking for the cluelessness of God by looking, in turn, for purely natural explanations. Good luck with that.

FOR YOUR ARSENAL

- Scientific findings can provide clues for whether God exists. This isn't surprising: the Bible says that we can see certain things about God through "the things that were made."

- Because we should expect the universe to look different if God exists, absence of evidence is, in this case, evidence of absence.

- God himself cannot be observed, so in the case of scientific evidence, his existence will have to be inferred. In other words, his existence will be a hypothesis based on observations.

EVOLUTION EXPLAINED?

IS EVOLUTION A NATURAL ALTERNATIVE?

So then, believers can expect scientists to find physical clues for God's existence. In fact, we have some candidates ready at hand. You're one. I'm another. There's no dearth of potential clues. Of course, if you and I can be explained *naturally*, we'll have to resign our candidacy. More generally, if there is an adequate natural explanation for the wanton complexity, order, and majesty we see in creation, then this wanton complexity, order, and majesty wouldn't necessarily be clues for God's existence.

And even if there's no natural explanation on the horizon, you won't find atheists stuffing God into the gap. Although that *could* happen. Just recently, British philosopher Antony Flew, a long-time proponent of atheism, announced that he had become a theist (but not a Christian). In a 2004 interview, he said, "I think that the most impressive arguments for God's existence are those that are supported by recent scientific discoveries. . . . The argument to Intelligent Design is enormously stronger than it was when I first met it."[1]

We shouldn't underestimate the power of the argument from design. But we should also be realistic. Humans, after all, no longer naturally wish there to be a God. We're all in need of repair.

The question, then, is, "*Is* there a decent natural explanation for life?" Darwin, I have heard, provided one. Philosopher of science Ronald Giere, for example, claims that, "By showing how species could evolve through natural processes, Darwin undercut projects for a natural theology based on an argument from design. The apparent design in nature is only apparent, so there is no basis for positing an intelligent designer."[2]

Is this true? Is evolution a sufficient or even decent alternative to divine design? This is a deep and interesting question. To make things manageable, I'll look at the most common attempt at a natural explanation. My conclusion will be that it isn't even in the neighborhood of decent.

I hope you'll agree.

THE EVOLUTION OF LIFE

We'll need to separate two issues. One is the evolution of more complicated forms of life from simpler forms. That is, once organisms have already appeared on earth, what accounts for their alleged progression to more elaborate organisms? The second issue is the very appearance of life from inorganic or nonliving matter—the *origin* of life, rather than its evolution.

Hereby separating the two issues, let's focus first on the evolution of organisms. That is, let's assume for now that we've taken care of the origins of life. Let's suppose further—to make things easier on atheists—that science does indeed provide unequivocal evidence that complex organisms have evolved from relatively simpler ones. Would such magnanimous aid help atheists provide a plausible natural explanation for such evolution?

It's difficult to see how. Even with our charity, atheists would still need to give us a good reason to believe that evolution is unguided, occurring entirely through the combined efforts of random mutation and natural selection. Does anyone have a good reason for believing that evolution is blind?

Whether good or not, here it is. Stenger says,

> There may indeed be more to the mechanism of evolution than random mutation and natural selection. It simply isn't intelligent design. Complex material systems exhibit a purely natural process called *self-organization* and this appears to occur in both living and nonliving systems.[3]

To show us that material objects really do organize themselves, Stenger draws our attention to the breathtaking double spiral pattern found in both sunflowers (living) and droplets of magnetic fluid on a film of oil (nonliving). These phenomena are mesmerizing. But Stenger goes and ruins the mood with his revelation that the double spiral is merely the minimization of potential energy—nothing but "simple physics."[4] The magic is gone. "In fact," he continues, "nothing is needed besides basic, purely reductionist physics and chemistry."[5] Talk about unweaving a rainbow.

But let us, again in an act of charity, allow Stenger his claim that these spirally occurrences are merely the result of natural laws. Sadly, even this isn't enough to help him. That's because he's trying to explain one case of apparent design by pointing to other cases of apparent design. The lawfulness of nature is nothing more than yet another example of the universe's astonishing complexity and order.

To be sure, if we already had a good reason to believe that the laws of physics themselves *weren't* the product of some cosmological engineer, that the celestial blueprints didn't spec out these laws, then perhaps Stenger would be onto something, something like an argument. And what might such a reason be? What evidence does Stenger have for his belief that the laws of physics themselves weren't designed?

He doesn't tell us, but I think he would say that he has *scientific* evidence. We've seen that a prevalent—perhaps the most prevalent—type of reasoning in (and out of) science is inference to the best explanation. Remember how it goes: given what you already know about the world, you decide what best explains some particular observation, some event or object. Perhaps Stenger's reasoning, then, is this: Given what we already know about the world, the best and ultimate explanation of the laws of physics is . . . is what? Is nothing, nothing at all. The laws of physics are brute facts. Explanations must eventually come to an end, so why not here? And even if there *is* some heretofore-undreamt-of explanation, "It simply isn't intelligent design."

But why think this? Or rather, why think that the best explanation of apparent design isn't genuine design? Now, if what we already know about the world includes that there's no designer, we could reasonably rule out intelligent design as a good explanation of nature's physical laws (and so as an explanation of complex organisms). But aside from already believing that there's no designer, it isn't even remotely evident that the explanation "simply isn't intelligent design."

So then, Stenger's claim—that the complexity of life isn't evidence of a designer—seems to depend on his belief that there is no designer. It takes very little effort to get where you want to go if you're already there, unless you travel in an immense circle. Maybe Stenger's strategy is to wear us down with a forced and lengthy march.

So, even if the laws of physics and chemistry could account for the evolution of life, we haven't been given a good reason to think so—at least we haven't been given reason to think that these laws are the result of blind chance. And it's plausible that the burden of proof is on anyone who wants to show that it is; after all, the default position is to see design everywhere in nature. Dawkins concedes this natural tendency: "Who, before Darwin, could have guessed that something so apparently *designed* as a dragonfly's wing or an eagle's eye was really the end product of a long sequence of non-random but purely natural causes."[6]

The answer is probably something like "no one." And it seems that even Darwin himself had his doubts, saying, unexpectedly, "From the . . . impossibility of conceiving this immense and wonderful universe . . . [as] the results of blind chance or necessity . . . I feel compelled to look to a First Cause having an intelligent mind in some degree analogous to that of man: and [therefore] I deserve to be called a Theist."[7] His doubts extend backward, to the beginning: as far as the first appearance of life, Darwin said, "It is mere rubbish, thinking at present of the origin of life; one might as well think of the origin of matter."[8]

But maybe it's no longer mere rubbish to think of the origin of life. It might even be worthwhile. So let's.

THE ORIGIN OF LIFE

Scientists concede that it's unlikely in the extreme for life to have formed from inorganic matter. In *The God Delusion*, Richard Dawkins writes, "The origin of life only had to happen once. We therefore can allow it to have been an extremely improbable event, many orders of magnitude more improbable than most people realize."[9]

And the improbability is staggering. British astronomer, mathematician, and atheist Fred Hoyle famously compared the possibility of life appearing from inorganic matter to the possibility that "a tornado sweeping through a junk-yard might assemble a Boeing 747 from the materials therein."[10] Hoyle dealt with the improbability in a surprising way. Jane Gregory reports that Hoyle believed "that the geological record showed that 'the Earth was showered with living cells from the very dawn of creation.' The interiors of comets were well suited to the initiation of life."[11]

Aliens. Terrestrial life began as alien life. And Hoyle wasn't the only scientist who believed this. Hitchens pointed out that the codiscoverer of the DNA molecule and Nobel Laureate Francis Crick "even allowed himself to flirt with the theory that life was 'inseminated' on earth by bacteria spread from a passing comet."[12]

Aliens, however, aren't a common explanation for terrestrial life. The explanation that most secular scientists give is that there are actually many different universes, perhaps an infinite number of them.

Surely, with an infinite number of universes, there is the distinct possibility that at least one of them—this one, for example—will be just right for life. Multiple universes (composing a "multiverse") are now all the rage. Even if the odds that life should have emerged from inorganic matter are astoundingly negligible, we can easily beat these odds by positing an *infinite* number of universes. Try not to think of infinity as simply a really big number; it's not a number at all. It is endless. No matter how small the odds are (as long as they aren't zero), an infinite number of chances can always get you where you want to go.

Now a multiverse is surely a better explanation than the anthropic principle we met earlier. For one thing, it's an actual explanation. But there are two problems with the multiverse explanation. The first is that there is, as yet, no physical evidence for one. The other problem stems from its adherents' motivation, specifically, their desire to avoid all the "cosmic coincidences."[13] To be sure, this desire doesn't mean there *isn't* a multiverse, but it would be nice to have some independent reasons to believe in it, reasons other than wanting there to be one (again, something like physical evidence).

Let us ignore that, though. Should a Christian be impressed by the multiverse explanation? To put it differently, what's a better explanation: that the universe was designed or that there are many, many universes? Well, that depends on whether you come to the decision as a believer or not. To put it differently, taking the multiverse seriously (or not) shows again that science isn't religiously neutral.

"PLEASE OH PLEASE LET IT BE TRUE!"

I've always wondered why an atheist would greet evolution with relief. It seems to me that if life evolved, then evolution would have to have been guided. And in that case, evolution would be just another argument for God's existence, just another argument for design.

But the clue lies, I think, in the apparent confidence of many recent atheists. If you only read *their* books, and not the vast literature on the argument from design, you would think that it has been a slam dunk for the atheists. Regarding the argument, and with a significant amount of swagger, Dawkins asserts,

> the mature Darwin blew [the argument from design] out of the water. There has probably never been a more devastating rout of popular belief by clever reasoning than Charles Darwin's destruction of the argument from design. It was so unexpected. Thanks to Darwin, it is no longer true to say that nothing that we know looks designed unless it is designed.[14]

Perhaps Dawkins really *is* this confident. If so, he's deluding himself about the strength of his evidence. Or maybe he's merely whistling in the dark. Maybe he's bluffing. Whatever the case, there's a lesson here. When you find out that someone so cocksure is so mistaken, you should watch him closely after that. A mistake is excusable; speaking so far beyond your evidence usually isn't. On this, atheists will agree; for this is exactly what they accuse believers of.

FOR YOUR ARSENAL

- The complexity of living organisms has always been seen as powerful evidence for a divine designer. But if there is a purely naturalistic explanation for the existence of living creatures, this evidence is nullified.

- When considering the merits of evolution, two issues must be kept separate: (1) the initial appearance of life from inorganic matter; (2) the evolution of organisms toward greater complexity.

- A common naturalistic explanation of the *origin* of life, given its immense improbability, is that there are many—perhaps an infinite number of—universes (the multiverse theory) and so it is reasonable to think that at least one of them would result in life. There is no physical evidence for the existence of these other universes.

- A common explanation for the *evolution* of organisms is that evolution is naturally caused by nothing more than fundamental laws of physics. Even if this were true, there is still the question of why the laws of physics are such that they result in evolution.

17

THE USER-FRIENDLY UNIVERSE

GOD'S SPOKEN WORLD

Although the faith-and-reason discussion spans millennia, it wasn't until the Enlightenment that the discussion became couched in terms that pitted science against religion. "Religion" and "science" have become synonyms for "faith" and "reason." The explanation isn't difficult to find: the Enlightenment was largely a self-conscious response to the Scientific Revolution of the previous century. The new science—Newtonian physics—seemed to have rescued Europe from its benighted reliance on faith and tradition. Science became the exemplar of rational inquiry.

An unprecedented explosion of enthusiasm followed, enthusiasm that approached fanaticism. In this heady atmosphere, Lord Byron composed a messianic ode to Newton. In it, it is Newton, not Christ, who reverses mankind's banishment from Eden (fruit seems to be a theme):

When Newton saw an apple fall, he found
In that slight startle from his contemplation—
'Tis said (for I'll not answer above ground
For any sage's creed or calculation)—
A mode of proving that the earth turn'd round
In a most natural whirl, called "gravitation;"
And this is the sole mortal who could grapple,
Since Adam, with a fall or with an apple.

A few French even began a religion around Newton. Had Newton known about such things, he would have died of an aneurysm rather than being killed by kidney stones.

But it's certainly true that Newton's work bordered on miraculous; his accomplishments were the fruition (fruit again) of the Scientific Revolution. In fact, they were the achievement of something much larger. Newton had fulfilled the dream of Greek philosophy, in particular, Plato's charge to his Academy to find a *mathematical description* of the heavens. This, Newton did in spades, going far beyond anything Plato had dreamed. He unified terrestrial and celestial phenomena, showing beyond doubt that there was—as Galileo had recognized—a single set of laws for the heavens and the earth. We finally had a *universe*—this one created by Newton. It's difficult to avoid the divine metaphors.

So the Scientific Revolution was a watershed event in the West's intellectual and cultural history, and it centered around one thing: the mathematical description of the cosmos. The revolution—the coup—overthrew Aristotle's entire science with *mathematics*.

Although Newton did much of the actual work, it was Galileo who began spreading Plato's gospel—the news that the world is mathematical. In a famous passage, he restated Plato's ancient idea:

Philosophy [i.e., natural philosophy or science] is written in this all-encompassing book that is constantly open before our eyes, that is the universe; but it cannot be understood unless one first learns to understand the language and knows the characters in which it is written. It is written in mathematical language, and its characters are triangles, circles, and other geometrical figures; without these it is humanly impossible to understand a word of it, and one wanders around pointlessly in a dark labyrinth.[1]

All the players in the Scientific Revolution believed that nature's language is fundamentally mathematical. Furthermore, they believed that its author is God. Johannes Kepler echoed Galileo's sentiments:

Thus God himself was too kind to remain idle, and began to play the game of signatures, signing his likeness into the world; therefore I chance to think that all nature and the graceful sky are symbolized in the art of geometry.[2]

It's a simple yet fertile idea: the mathematical nature of the universe is evidence of divine design. Mathematics is God's signature—what we earlier called his fingerprints. When God spoke creation into existence, the language he used was fundamentally mathematical, even if not solely so. A terrifying thought for mathphobes everywhere.

THE FIRST ENLIGHTENMENT

The roots of Western culture—its Greek roots anyway—are in what has been called the "First Western Enlightenment." The first person to see the light, as far as we know—the West's first philosopher—was Thales of Miletus. Thales was also the first scientist, and a mathematician to boot. But this is only because math, science, and philosophy still formed a single discipline, as they ought. We can't understand these three disciplines unless we understand them all.

Thales inaugurated the First Western Enlightenment by explaining natural phenomena *naturally*, without appealing to the traditional Homeric gods. Nature, Thales believed, could explain itself. And

Thales's ultimate explanation was—and I'm not kidding—water. According to Thales, a single unifying substance explained all the variation and complexity of the cosmos. Today the fundamental building blocks of the universe are quarks, which come in six "flavors" (still not kidding). And scientists discovered quarks, by the way, while blindfolded, being led entirely by mathematics.

One of Thales's pupils was the famous mystic and mathematician Pythagoras—after whom we have named the famous triangle theorem. Pythagoras, God love him, should be more famous than that. He's woefully underappreciated. Pythagoras's great idea—and the reason why more children should be named "Pythagoras"—was that the entire universe is literally composed, not of water, but of numbers. The Pythagorean motto was *All is number*; and though literally false, it inspired a sort of religious brotherhood.

The most influential member of the Pythagorean brotherhood (which included sisters) is also the most influential philosopher of all time: the great Plato. The history of philosophy, it is said, is but a mere footnote to Plato. And there's a good deal of truth to this. Plato identified all the main issues, gave ingenious answers, and generally set the agenda for Western philosophy, as well as for science. As we saw, this agenda was to describe the world mathematically. After all—it bears repeating—Plato believed that the universe was fundamentally mathematical, that the patterns or templates of the cosmos could be reduced to mathematical objects like numbers and geometric shapes. So strong was Plato's faith in the Pythagorean creed that, in Plato's ideal government, the leaders would all be philosophers who had studied nothing but mathematics for ten years straight.

Plato also thought that democracy was a terrible idea.

PYTHAGOREANISM COMES TRUE

Notice that both enlightenments—the first *and* the second—are characterized by a rejection of traditional supernatural accounts of nature. In each case, reason supplanted religion. And the point here is that reason—in both enlightenments—was ultimately manifested by mathematics, of all things. This is surprising because our only encounters with mathematics have been through dry methods of calculation. But it's easy to see why mathematics is a manifestation of reason; it's something for which you need only your mind. Of course, you might need something to write with, but only as an aid to memory and keeping things straight. Mathematics is pure reason.

We take for granted that we can apply mathematics—something done entirely with the mind—to the study of the *physical* world. What could be more natural, we now believe, than to use mathematics in science? But the fact that we do is pure magic and has intrigued philosophers, scientists, and mathematicians since the beginning. And the mystery deepens as modern physics becomes almost purely mathematical. Einstein—who discovered his theories of relativity by following mathematics instead of observations—said, "At this point an enigma presents itself which in all ages has agitated inquiring minds. How can it be that mathematics, being after all a product of human thought which is independent of experience, is so admirably appropriate to the objects of reality?"[3] Einstein isn't alone in his appreciation of this enigma. The physicist and Nobel Laureate Steven Weinberg says that "it is positively spooky how the physicist finds the mathematician has been there before him or her."[4] Richard Feynman, another Nobel Prize winner, said, "I find it quite amazing that it is possible to predict what will happen by mathematics, which is simply following rules which really have nothing to do with the original thing."[5]

Perhaps the most famous remarks come from Nobel Laureate physicist Eugene Wigner, in his fascinating article "The Unreasonable Effectiveness of Mathematics in the Natural Sciences." He concluded the essay with these words:

> The miracle of the appropriateness of the language of mathematics for the formulation of the laws of physics is a wonderful gift which we neither understand nor deserve. We should be grateful

for it and hope that it will remain valid in future research and that it will extend, for better or for worse, to our pleasure, even though perhaps also to our bafflement, to wide branches of learning.[6]

Pythagoras was apparently on to something. The late mathematician Morris Kline pointed out that the Scientific Revolution was founded upon the following "Pythagorean" principles:

1. The universe is ordered by perfect mathematical laws.
2. Divine reason is the organizer of nature.
3. Human reason can discern the divine pattern.[7]

The Pythagorean faith continues today (although in a heretical form: the "divine" part has been largely forgotten). From Pythagoras to Plato to Galileo to Newton to Einstein, scientists and philosophers have believed that nature is rational, and that this rationality is fundamentally mathematical. And if there weren't such a felicitous fit between our minds and the world, we'd never have made it so far in physics. We'd never have made it at all.

Today mathematics reaches far beyond the realm of physics. Mathematical structures constantly show up unexpected and therefore unannounced. Wigner famously shared a story

about two friends, who were classmates in high school, talking about their jobs. One of them became a statistician and was working on population trends. He showed a reprint to his former classmate. The reprint started, as usual, with the Gaussian distribution and the statistician explained to his former classmate the meaning of the symbols for the actual population, for the average population, and so on. His classmate was a bit incredulous and was not quite sure whether the statistician was pulling his leg. "How can you know that?" was his query. "And what is this symbol here?" "Oh," said the statistician, "this is pi." "What is that?" "The ratio of the circumference of the circle to its diameter." "Well, now you are pushing your joke too far," said the classmate, "surely the population has nothing to do with the circumference of the circle."[8]

Pi, or Π (which stands for the endless number 3.14159265 . . .), is the ratio of any circle's circumference to its diameter. This ratio was discovered millennia before the discovery of the statistical formula for populations. Moreover—and this is the real mystery—it was discovered in a context that couldn't be more different from the population of organisms.

Such felicity happens more frequently than you might expect. And like the fine-tuning of the universe for the existence of life, it would be nice to have an explanation for it. But Wigner said that this "enormous usefulness of mathematics in the natural sciences is something bordering on the mysterious and that there is no rational explanation for it."[9] Not only is it a mystery, but one wrapped in an enigma and containing a riddle. The reasonableness of the universe seems itself unreasonable.

If you're looking for a purely natural explanation.

IT JUST GETS WEIRDER

As physics grows, mathematics' unreasonable effectiveness becomes more pronounced. Philosopher Mark Steiner argues in his recent book, *The Applicability of Mathematics as a Philosophical Problem,* that the use of math in contemporary physics simply doesn't make sense unless the universe is human centered. The universe is too intellectually "user-friendly," too ergonomic, to be an accident. It fits our cognitive faculties too well, uncannily conforming to our unique way of thinking.

But Steiner's impressive study shows that scientists use mathematics for more than merely *describing* nature—as astounding as that use is. In addition, he points out, mathematics allows physicists to *discover* new phenomena, not merely to describe things we already knew about. And these discoveries, argues Steiner—discoveries at the center of relativity and quantum mechanics—are inexplicable for those who think the universe is indifferent to mankind's "goals and values."[10]

Steiner's examples are taken from the time when scientists were first trying to describe the atomic and subatomic world. There are two things to realize about the atomic and subatomic realm. First, we cannot observe atoms; they are forever beyond our ken of observation. Moreover, and this is the second thing, atoms don't behave anything at all like ordinary garden-variety objects. When most of us think of an atom, we imagine a minuscule solar system, with electrons orbiting a central nucleus. This picture, unfortunately, is entirely wrong. In fact, we have no accurate way to picture or visualize atoms and their behavior. All our metaphors quickly break down. Subatomic particles—if they can be called "particles" in any recognizable sense—don't simultaneously have a location *and* speed, only one or the other. Furthermore, they at times behave like waves, at other times like particles, and in any case, they seem to be "smeared" rather than distinctly located.

These two facts—that the atomic realm is unobservable and that it fails to behave like the familiar macro-world—put the issue into sharp relief. At the end of the 1800s, physicists were stymied, and it seemed to them that atomic physics was reduced to blind guessing.[11] Direct observations were out. Nor could physicists use familiar mathematics to derive new atomic laws. Existing mathematical laws governed objects and phenomena that behave fundamentally different from the ones physicists were trying to investigate. This difference between the macroscopic and microscopic realms was simply too great to rely on physical similarities. So it's difficult to see how mathematics could help guide the physicist here.

But they used it anyway. And it worked.

FEEL THE MAGIC

So, how *do* physicists use mathematics as a guide, as eyes to see into the atom? There are different ways, all nearly unbelievable, except that they're successful.

One way is to still trust the mathematics from the observable realm and tinker with it until you come upon something that seems to work. Not only does this require a fair amount of conjecture and gut feeling, but the gut feeling is of the mathematics, not the physical situation.

The general procedure is to assume that the unobservable realm behaves like the ordinary observable realm—a false assumption. Then take an equation governing the observable realm and assume that this will—with some tinkering—describe the unobservable, quantum realm. The old classical equations are then converted by merely manipulating the *symbols* of the equation, without having a physical basis for doing so. In other words, the new equation often doesn't have any physical meaning at all; the physicist is just using symbols, hoping they'll give insight into the quantum realm. Steiner calls this sort of symbolic manipulation "magical" because physicists are studying the symbols of the mathematical language rather than physical objects, thereby confusing the symbols with reality.[12]

One example that Steiner gives is the discovery of a new particle, the positron (essentially an electron with a positive charge). The English physicist Paul Dirac first developed an equation that governed the microscopic realm using the above "magical" method.[13] That in itself is spooky. This new equation gave several solutions. (Solutions to an equation are just those numbers that, when plugged into the empty variables, keep the equation balanced—that keep both sides of the equal sign the same.) But there were solutions that didn't seem to correspond to any real physical situation. That is, when plugging particular values into the equation's variables, the resulting solved version of the equation seemed to describe a curious physical world, one that couldn't exist. Normally, therefore, these solutions would have been considered "impossible."[14] Nevertheless, Dirac supposed that the weird solved version of the equation might correspond to reality, trusting pure mathematics to guide him.[15] Beyond all hope, he was right.

In another example—this one from general relativity—Steiner describes how black holes were "discovered." As one of the variables in the equations goes to a certain value, another goes to infinity. Steiner says that this solution would have ordinarily been ignored because it physically corresponded to a "singularity" in space-time itself, an "object" of infinite density and zero volume. Steiner continues, "Nevertheless, scientists had enough faith in the equation to believe in even this solution."[16] Again, the solved equation—like a mystical oracle—told physicists of an object that was unlike anything they had imagined. "Scientists," Steiner says, "are now persuaded of the actual existence of black holes."[17]

It would be difficult to think of a more appropriate word than "magic."

WHAT ON EARTH *IS* MATHEMATICS?

Why should the universe help us out, letting us use such methods to uncover its hidden nature? These methods seem to put humans in a privileged place among the universe, as if the universe wanted us to learn about it. Our sense of the problem becomes even more heightened if Steiner is right when he says that the concept of mathematics itself is a human-dependent concept.[18]

Steiner notes that it's up to the mathematician as to what counts as a mathematical structure. Chess, too, has a structure, for example, but mathematicians don't typically consider it mathematical.[19] Why not?

One clue is that many mathematical concepts are developed long before they have any known application. In fact, mathematicians usually come up with new concepts without any thought of whether they correspond to physical reality. This raises the question, then: Why study mathematics? Isn't mathematics simply a tool to help us investigate the universe? Not if you ask mathematicians. The reason why mathematicians study mathematics isn't simply "because math works." In fact, most mathematics is never applicable in that sense at all; it's purely theoretical.

Rather, a much more common answer to why mathematicians study math is that the mathematical realm is simply and uniquely beautiful. The famous mathematician G. H. Hardy said,

> The mathematician's patterns, like the painter's or the poet's, must be *beautiful*; the ideas, like the colours or the words, must fit together in a harmonious way. Beauty is the first test: there is no permanent place in the world for ugly mathematics. . . .
> It may be very hard to *define* mathematical beauty, but that is just as true of beauty of any kind—we may not know quite what we mean by a beautiful poem, but that does not prevent us from recognizing one when we read it.[20]

Similarly, Eugene Wigner said that most of the more esoteric mathematical concepts (like imaginary numbers) were developed because they "are apt subjects on which the mathematician can demonstrate his ingenuity and sense of formal beauty."[21]

If, as Steiner says, "Concepts are selected as mathematical because they foster beautiful theorems and beautiful theories," then "modern mathematics expresses the human aesthetic sense."[22] Mathematical concepts, according to Steiner, aren't developed by looking at the world. Rather, they're developed by looking at ourselves in some sense. It is the mathematicians' own sense of what is beautiful that identifies which concepts are mathematical, not whether these concepts are useful for exploring the physical world. But then it seems that these concepts could be applicable—could give us truths about the physical world—only if humans have some special connection to the universe. And this connection seems to be more than a mere physical connection; it seems like something much more eerie.

If it's true that humans are a special part of the universe, this would fly in the face of atheism. According to atheism, after all, we're nothing more than accidental chunks of physical matter, like rocks, only more active. By using mathematics the way they do, atheist physicists act contrary to their core beliefs about themselves. We sometimes call this sort of inconsistency between actions and beliefs "irrational."

MATHEMATICS EXPLAINED?

But maybe there's a perfectly good naturalistic explanation, one that accounts for the "unreasonable effectiveness of mathematics" using only the resources of blind, unguided evolution. Consider the claim that natural selection has sifted our cognitive faculties for mathematical concepts that work on nature. It would be beneficial, after all, to know how many elk are in that herd, and how many hunters you'll need in order to have a decent chance of killing enough to feed the folks back home. Knowing how to count might come in handy.[23] Although the range of mathematical concepts needed for sheer survival is small indeed, suppose there are enough to get mathematics going. Would we then have a decent evolutionary explanation for the types of mathematical discoveries we find in twentieth-century physics?

Not likely. In fact, according to Steiner, given evolution, we should expect humans to be entirely unable to discover laws having no bearing on survival. Even Dawkins concedes that "we never evolved to navigate the world of atoms," rather, "our brains have evolved to help our bodies find their way around the world on the scale at which those bodies operate."[24]

Evolution then seems to have left us wholly unprepared for particle physics. For one thing, the discoveries of contemporary physics are not only about phenomena that are *forever* unobservable (no matter how good our instruments are, we can never detect some of these); these phenomena also behave radically different from the world that allegedly governed our ancestors' cognitive development. And so this explanation doesn't even seem to accord with evolutionary theory itself.

Not only are the cognitive environments different; the mathematics that physicists use isn't merely simple arithmetic and geometry. The mathematical concepts in question—the ones employed to make discoveries in modern physics—are often far more complex.[25] Simple concepts like basic arithmetic and geometry can *perhaps* be explained naturally. That is, maybe there's a plausible argument for the claim that number concepts, for example, fundamentally aid in the survival of a species. I actually doubt this, but if so, there would still be a chasm between elementary math and that used for contemporary physics. (And notice that I'm entirely ignoring the evolutionary reasons we had for doubting the reliability of our cognitive faculties in the first place.)

Again, doesn't there seem to be a special connection between humans and the universe? Mathematicians can follow their private mental concepts, concepts that, despite originating inside them, point to new and unbelievable truths about a world outside of them (and far beyond the ken of sense perception). And doesn't it also seem plausible that this ability is the result of divine design?

Not to everyone. Victor Stenger claims that, to him, "the universe and life do not look at all designed; they look just as they would be expected to look if they were not designed at all."[26] But remember that there's a difference between the universe merely *looking* designed and *being* designed. And nearly everyone agrees that it looks designed. In fact, the entire debate assumes this; the real controversy is over whether the appearance is only skin deep.

It seems, however, that there's still no decent natural explanation for the unreasonable effectiveness of math. At least by all appearances.

FOR YOUR ARSENAL

- Because mathematics is responsible for the Scientific Revolution, which is, in turn, responsible for the Enlightenment and the evidentialist objection, mathematics is central to the debate between belief and unbelief.

- Despite giving rise to the evidentialist objection, the Scientific Revolution was founded on the belief that God designed the world mathematically. In fact, this belief goes back to the beginning of Western intellectual history, to Plato and Pythagoras.

- Mathematics has become increasingly important to the development of contemporary physics, guiding scientists where observation cannot go. There is no naturalistic explanation for this user-friendliness of the universe, for the "unreasonable effectiveness of mathematics."

18

THE RELUCTANT
SUPERNATURALIST

Mathematics, surprisingly, cuts right to the heart of the matter. It was, we saw, responsible for the Scientific Revolution, the mathematical coup that brought down Aristotle's two-thousand-year rule over science. The Scientific Revolution, in turn, inaugurated the Enlightenment and its rationalistic excesses, of which we can count the evidentialist objection to belief in God. Mathematics, therefore, might look like the source of our problems.

Yet, despite being the impetus of the Enlightenment's declaration of freedom from religious superstition and authority, mathematics actually suggests the existence of God. This is sweet irony. But the debates over design today center almost exclusively on biological examples, rather than on those of contemporary physics. Nevertheless, we saw that scientists attempt to ultimately explain evolution—albeit unsuccessfully—with physics' mathematical laws.

But there is another way mathematics enters the debate over God's existence, and this will again suggest that mathematics is central to

Western philosophy. The story begins with Plato, not surprisingly, and ends with the most famous American philosopher of the twentieth century. The plot revolves around what may be the main question of philosophy, depending on your temperament. In fact, the story itself might be one of the most important in contemporary philosophy. But no one outside of philosophy has even heard of it.

THOSE GUYS AGAIN?

By the 1950s, traditional philosophy was dead. The logical positivists had killed it. Recall that the logical positivists were enamored with the twentieth century's revolutionary advancements in physics, mathematics, and logic, and they wanted some of *that* for philosophy. Let's, they said, make philosophy more like these disciplines—more scientific, more mathematical, and more logical.

After all, philosophers had gotten basically nowhere since Plato and were still arguing over the same issues. Western philosophy was nothing but a series of footnotes to Plato, which is just a polite way of saying that philosophy had stagnated for over two thousand years. Plato raised some curious questions, to be sure, but apparently humans weren't adept at coming up with the answers. This showed, the logical positivists believed, that these perennial philosophical questions were mere pseudo-questions—they looked like questions but were really literally meaningless. Philosophers had been "bewitched" by language, as Wittgenstein might say. Traditional philosophy was the result of a trick, a linguistic sleight of hand.

This was the sad state of philosophy in the middle of the last century. But the logical positivist's new doctrines weren't any better than those of traditional philosophy (worse, in fact), and they would soon go the way of all flesh. One of the philosophers responsible for the logical positivist's downfall was entirely sympathetic with their goal: to make philosophy more like science.

QUINE AND NATURALISM

Willard Van Orman Quine ("Van" to his friends) received his PhD in philosophy from Harvard in the 1930s and spent his life teaching at the distinguished university, even contributing to its distinction. By the time he died in 2000, he had helped change large swaths of the philosophical terrain. Throughout his career, he worked to create a philosophy that would be continuous with empirical science, producing highly technical work that combined philosophy with math, logic, and science.

Quine believed that our best going theory of the world is science, specifically physics. Anything worth knowing can be known by science, and so any philosophy would have to be somehow part of the scientific endeavor. He is famous for saying, in his typically quotable way, "Philosophy of science is philosophy enough."[1]

Quine didn't think that science was infallible, but he did think more highly of it than any other way of discovery. But on religion, he once wrote, "What my own philosophy can say about God is that there is no such thing, at any rate in any ordinary sense of the word; and there is no answering for extraordinary senses. I am not a religious man."[2]

Plantinga once told me that he and Quine had spent some time together in the old days (it was at a conference, if I recall correctly); in characteristic understatement, Plantinga put it this way: "Quine wasn't particularly impressed with religion." In any case, Quine was a philosophical naturalist, someone who believes that the natural world is all there is.[3] For Quine, there was nothing outside of space and time, nothing supernatural.

But I want to argue that Quine's singular devotion to the natural realm led him straight into a philosophy that countenanced—indeed depended on—a supernatural realm, a world outside of nature. And though he said very little about his philosophy's implications, it was clear that he wasn't entirely pleased.

PHILOSOPHY'S MOST FAMOUS THEORY

Plato's greatest doctrine is his theory of the Forms. It is, I daresay, the most popular theory in all of philosophy. Its importance is matched only by its weirdness. In fact, almost no one wants to believe it if they don't have to. Peter van Inwagen says, "It would be better not to believe in [Forms] if we could get away with it."[4] But the theory's other salient characteristic is that it is almost impossible to avoid; that is, philosophers are forced into believing it. And so van Inwagen also laments that, even though it would be best not to believe in Plato's Forms, "We can't get away with it."[5] But philosophers don't usually come into Plato's fold quietly. Quine himself put up one of the noblest fights in history against the doctrine. He succumbed nevertheless.

What are Forms, and why do philosophers find them so distasteful? And why are they so recalcitrant?

Plato, being the observant fellow he was, noticed that a red apple and a red rose have something in common: they're both red. In fact, all red things share this. Similarly, all circular things have something in common. We say that objects that share such properties are *similar*. Plato was nothing if not meticulous.

This began innocently enough, but Plato would open a Pandora's box. He just *had* to know what makes these objects similar. His answer is startling. He said that red things are similar in virtue of redness. (There's more.) This redness is the *thing* that red things hold in common. (Wait for it . . .) Plato said there was a single object in virtue of which all red things were red. This shared object is the Form of the Red or the Form of Redness. After all, when we say "The rose is red" and "The apple is red," the word "red" must refer to the same thing, and that thing, said Plato, is a Form. The word "red" must refer to some*thing* after all, if sentences like "The rose is red" are true; it's not as if we're talking about *nothing*. (Perhaps you now see why the logical positivists thought that much of philosophy is little more than doodling with words.)

I trust that it's rather easy to think of a rose as an object, as a thing. But what about the color red? How is that a thing? To be sure, there are red *things*, like apples, roses, and fire engines. But these aren't the *color*. According to Plato, however, the Form of Redness, the Form of Circularity (the thing that all circular objects share), and the Form of Dogginess (the thing that all dogs share) are genuine objects. They aren't, to be sure, located in space and time; we couldn't *find* them. Neither are they made of matter; they're not something we could touch. In fact, they aren't made of anything, really. Moreover, these Forms are eternal and unchanging. Much else it's hard to say. But we can say this: they don't exist in nature; they're outside of nature, or *supernatural*. In fact, the realm of the Forms—where all the Forms reside—is called "Plato's Heaven."

Very mysterious indeed, which is why many philosophers have wished to avoid Platonic Forms at nearly any cost. And nearly none of them could. Maybe this is inevitable. Perhaps no one can ever avoid including some sort of mysterious objects in his or her philosophy.

Aristotle, Plato's most famous pupil, wasn't one to take philosophy's most famous theory lying down. As much as Aristotle respected his master, he disagreed just as much. Aristotle believed in Forms all right, but he wanted them out of Plato's heaven and down here on earth, in the world we can touch. So he placed these Forms in the physical objects themselves. The fire engine, the apple, the rose all "contain" the Form of the Red. Now I'm not going to try to make sense of Aristotle's view, since there's no consensus about what Aristotle himself believed. After all, his writings are really lecture notes. Despite the ambiguity of Aristotle's resistance to Plato's Forms, it inspired centuries of philosophers and theologians to take up the cause.

And so this debate over Platonic Forms took center stage for much of Western philosophy's history. Philosophers of the Middle Ages took the debate to new levels of sophistication, often making their highly technical philosophy entirely inscrutable. Remember, however, the fundamental concern is as simple as it is prevalent: Exactly why are things similar?

The Scientific Revolution and the ensuing Enlightenment doused the debate with cold water, with philosophers turning their attention to the exciting discoveries about the physical world. By the time the logical positivists reared their heads in the twentieth century, Plato's theory of Forms was all but dormant. In fact, as we saw, the logical positivists tried to banish most of philosophy's traditional questions. Philosophy was a pathetic and withered reflection of its former self.

But Quine would put new life into the old philosophy. Although I'm not sure he meant to.

DOING STRANGE THINGS WITH WORDS

Logical positivists tried to shut down philosophy by claiming that much of what we say about religion, ethics, and traditional philosophy is literally meaningless. This put philosophers on edge, making them much more careful with their words. Finally.

So, the logical positivists goaded their colleagues to study the logic of language. The new technical tools of mathematical logic—one of the things that had so excited the logical positivists in the first place—allowed philosophers to search beneath a sentence's surface for genuine linguistic meaning. And who could argue with that? After all, if we have been tricked into thinking that mere verbal quarrels are substantive philosophical issues, then the quicker we recognize when language is leading us astray, the better.

During this "linguistic turn" in philosophy, philosophers noticed that we really do some strange things with words. Simple and ordinary sentences—sentences that we effortlessly understand—actually perform feats of grammatical and semantic daring. Such feats are usually transparent to us; we're just too close to the language, too good at it. (In fact—and this is a relevant aside—we seem to come equipped with a linguistic cognitive faculty. Psychologists and cognitive scientists simply cannot account for our linguistic dexterity. It's a wonder we ever learn such a complex and subtle system of communication. The famous linguist and philosopher Noam Chomsky, for example, marveled at how, with our very haphazard, almost random, teaching, humans quickly develop the ability to use a language that far exceeds the quality of that training. He called this the "poverty of the stimulus"—garbage in, treasure out. Our linguistic ability is actually some of the most neglected evidence for design. In any case, we can add a language module to our list of cognitive faculties.)

One strange thing that philosophers noticed is just how frequently sentences seemed to refer to things that don't seem to be things at all. Philosophers were familiar, of course, with references to things like "red" and "circularity," things that Platonists had alleged were Forms. That had always been bad enough. But now, under further scrutiny, sentences seemed to refer to more besides. We all know, for example, that Santa Claus is fat. But we also know (now) that Santa doesn't exist. Therefore, philosophers reasoned, the word "Santa" must refer to something; after all, the term isn't meaningless. It can't be empty.

This, of course, is the type of issue that gives philosophers a bad name. In fact, this was exactly the kind of linguistic red herring that logical positivists were trying to expunge from philosophy. But this puzzle would have far-reaching consequences, which is exactly what makes it a good philosophical problem. A simple, childlike question that reminds us that the world is stranger than we thought.

In any case, this frivolous-looking problem fostered a huge movement in philosophy, one that would require all the logical resources that philosophers could throw at it. The reason is, terms that seemed to refer to a nonexistent entity seemed to require something like Platonic Forms. There didn't seem to be any way around it. The word "Santa" certainly didn't refer to a flesh-and-blood person; but neither does it refer to nothing. And this is when philosophers dusted off Plato's doctrine of the Forms. The word "Santa," philosophers said, refers to a Platonic Form, an object that exists in neither space nor time nor space-time (now that we have relativity). And to add insult to injury, this issue of nonexistent entities—the "problem of nonbeing"—seemed to be just another footnote to Plato. Would philosophy ever go anywhere?

But philosophers began to see ways around these new Platonic objects; they began to argue that there was really no need for the mysterious Forms. We can, they said, make sense of our language; we can keep these sentences true while removing the requirement for unnatural objects. I will skip the details—the subject requires concepts from logic that we simply aren't equipped to deal with here. But we can still understand the general strategy. Philosophers were able to escape the need for Platonic Forms by paraphrasing sentences like "Santa is fat" into new (and complicated) sentences that capture "what we really mean" by the original, while avoiding reference to Platonic Forms. Just as we can paraphrase "He lost his head" into something like "He was extremely angry," so, too, philosophers could paraphrase away reference to spooky objects like Forms.[6] Things were looking up.

And Quine played an important role in finding the solution. After all, he was an expert in logic, having made important contributions to the subject. He had the right skill set. He was hired on the spot.

Q: WHAT IS THERE? A: NUMBERS

Two things were happening simultaneously in philosophy, with Quine deeply involved in both. The first—and most significant—was a Renaissance of traditional philosophy. Historically, the problem of Platonic Forms had been one of *the* philosophical questions. And it was, in fact, part of a larger question, Quine pointed out: What is there? What sorts of things exist? This simple question occupied most of Western philosophy for millennia. The "what is there?" question was back on the table.

The second thing had to do with the *answer* to the "what is there?" question. Specifically, it looked as though there might not be Platonic Forms after all, with their ethereal and disquieting existence. And that was good news to most philosophers. Thanks to the tools of modern logic, it looked as though the age-old debate over the Forms was nearly over.

I should point out that these logical tools had actually been developed by mathematicians in order to deal with a crisis in mathematics, one that left math in near total and exciting disarray, where it remains, without the exciting part. In fact, the crisis led to a revolution that had far-reaching implications about what humans can know. We'll have to ignore it, unfortunately. But one of the salutary results of the revolution was the new and powerful logic that allowed philosophers to tackle the old Forms debate. Mathematics to the rescue again.

But any celebrating would have to wait—a long time, maybe forever.

Quine, we saw, was completely captivated by science. Yet to plumb the deep structure of the physical world, mathematics would have to guide us. We saw that in contemporary physics, scientists have had to rely less and less on observation and experiment and follow mathematics' lead.

Not surprisingly, many fundamental theories in physics are stated entirely in the language of mathematics. And Quine believed—not unreasonably—that our scientific theories are true, or generally true. Sure, they aren't infallible; to err is human, after all, and science is a paradigmatically human endeavor. It is one of the humanities. Nevertheless, if anything is true, science is. But, Quine pointed out, many of the sentences in physics refer to mathematical objects like numbers, functions, vectors, and Hilbert spaces. And, he reluctantly argued, the only way for such sentences to be true is for these objects to exist. If they didn't exist, then physics would be lying to us, telling us that there *are* mathematical objects. In other words, the truth of physics implies that there *really are* numbers, functions, vectors, and the like. Mathematical objects exist.

This would be positively horrible news for anyone wishing to avoid Platonic Forms—mathematical objects are Platonic Forms *in excelsis*. Plato himself populated his heaven with an infinite number of them. In fact, some scholars say that in Plato's later years, he reduced all of the Forms to mathematical ones. He kept the Pythagorean faith.

Quine would rather reject it. So he made a valiant attempt to paraphrase sentences from physics to new sentences that referred only to physical objects and no mathematical ones. He quickly realized that this was impossible. In fact, he and other philosophers pointed out that our current scientific theories absolutely must refer to mathematical objects, to Platonic Forms. Mathematical objects are indispensable to science; we can't do science without them.[7]

Quine eventually gave up trying to avoid Platonic Forms, albeit very begrudgingly. He found himself stuck with the existence of mysterious mathematical objects. He called himself a "reluctant Platonist."

A TASTE FOR DESERT LANDSCAPES

You might wonder what all the fuss is about. Isn't mathematics just about ideas? After all, math is something we do entirely with our minds. Why think that numbers have to be Platonic Forms—eternal and unchanging objects that exist (somehow) outside of space and time?

There are actually very good reasons. When we say, for example, that there are three (whole) numbers between 1 and 5, we're saying something that's true whether or not anyone is thinking about it. (We're talking about numbers, not *numerals*; numerals only stand for numbers, just like your name merely stands for you.) And it would have been true that there are three numbers between 1 and 5 if humans had never existed, and would still be true if humans went extinct. It has been true from all eternity and will be true for all time. And if it is eternally true that there are three numbers between 1 and 5, then it is eternally true that there are numbers (at least three of them, those between 1 and 5). Again, this is the case regardless of whether there are any human minds, much less ideas in those minds. So numbers can't be ideas in our heads (and could your brain really store that many ideas?). To be sure, we can have ideas *about* numbers, just as we have ideas about deserts, dogs, and donkeys. But numbers themselves—and mathematical objects in general—aren't human ideas.

You can understand why Quine would be so reluctant to believe in numbers—and Platonic Forms in general. If you were a hard-core naturalist, fervently believing that there is no supernatural realm, you, too, would be reluctant to countenance a world of mysterious, eternal, unchanging objects. After all, you believe that there isn't *anything* beyond nature—nothing *super*natural. Furthermore, you would be quite vexed to discover that it was your adherence to naturalism that drove you to supernaturalism. On the one hand, it was physics that had convinced you that there's no supernatural realm in the first place; now you hear it telling you that there *is* something outside the natural world. And after all these years. You think you know someone.

Quine's initial doubt about the existence of Platonic Forms wasn't a disinterested skepticism. He famously said that he had a "taste for desert landscapes." That is, he would have preferred to believe in a sparse world of only matter, rather than in a lush reality filled with additional objects. This is really just a version of the famous Ockham's razor principle, which says that we shouldn't believe in any more objects than is necessary. Ockham's razor shaves away any useless entities, leaving the world soft and smooth. In fact, Quine called the perennial problem of Platonic objects "Plato's beard." Plato's beard, Quine quipped, had repeatedly dulled Ockham's razor.

SCIENCE WORKS BEST WITH SUPERNATURALISM

Recall that we began with one of the most central and enduring problems of Western philosophy—the problem of Platonic Forms. The Scientific Revolution seemed, for the time being, to put the kibosh on the discussion, and the logical positivists tried to bury traditional philosophy altogether. Philosophy, they said, should become more like science. This would make perfect sense if the only things that exist are those science can study. But in an unexpected series of events (unfortunate for some, not so much for others), the emphasis on science and its limited domain gave new life to traditional philosophy. Science seemed to open the door to a reality outside nature, outside its purported limits. In fact, the very thing that initiated the Scientific Revolution—mathematics—was the very thing that seemed to show that there were objects outside the natural realm. The strongest argument for Platonic Forms is from mathematics. Plato would be quite pleased.

Now, I want to suggest a moral here: naturalism leads to supernaturalism. That is, the physical world of space and time simply doesn't have the resources to support itself. We simply have to believe in something outside of the physical cosmos. Perhaps many things. But of course, that's exactly what atheists like Quine want to avoid. Stenger, for example, believes that "we need not include anything beyond matter . . . to describe the universe and its contents."[8] But describing the universe with physics requires the existence of numbers and other mathematical objects. And these objects are far "beyond matter."

So then, natural science works best with supernaturalism. Natural science itself has told us so.

ISN'T MATH DIVINE?

Christians have always felt the strength of the Forms. They have also realized that believing in objects that are somehow eternal and unchangeable poses a potential problem. Plantinga describes the situation: "God hasn't *created* the numbers; a thing is created only if its existence had a beginning, and no number ever began to exist."[9] This is because numbers and other mathematical objects have always existed. But how could there be eternal objects that God can neither create nor destroy? Does he have *any* control over them? Do they exist independently of him, eternally outside of his control?[10]

These are imminently reasonable questions. Augustine of Hippo's response—and that of many Christian philosophers after him—was to transform Plato's theory of the Forms, to make the

Forms "obscurely, *part* of God—perhaps identical with his intellect."[11] That is, the so-called Platonic Forms—including numbers, functions, and all the rest—are really divine ideas, and therefore eternal, unchangeable, and dependent upon God. Mathematics would be about ideas after all, just not about *human* ideas.

So, if you think that physics is largely true, then you have a decent argument for God's existence. Plantinga makes the following suggestion: "Mathematics thus takes its proper place as one of the *loci* of theology; perhaps this explains the high esteem in which it is held in many quarters."[12] Not in all quarters, unfortunately. Nevertheless, although most of us have done our very best to avoid mathematics, we now find that it was our friend all along. We need no longer take the existence of math as evidence for hell. Just the opposite. Mathematics gives ample evidence that there must be something beyond nature, something supernatural. Quine was vexed by this inconvenient truth. Furthermore, mathematics seems to suggest more than the mere existence of a supernatural realm; its uncanny applicability in science makes the universe look remarkably like it was made for us—and us for it.

Our dislike and fear of math, however, stems from learning only the mechanics and recipes for calculation, rather than the amazing underpinnings and implications of this marvelous and ubiquitous discipline. Although I have much to say regarding math education, this isn't the place. My point now—expressed in a question—is simply this: Who would have thought that mathematics was so central to it all? I suspect that even most mathematicians haven't.

And speaking of mathematics, it is now time we turned to the closely related topic of pain and suffering, what is known as the "problem of evil," the so-called Achilles' heel of Christianity. After all, I think we have cast enough doubt on the claim that science has shown there is no God.

FOR YOUR ARSENAL

- The Harvard philosopher and logician W. V. Quine resuscitated traditional philosophy by reviving Plato's theory of the Forms.

- Quine was a naturalist—he believed that there is no supernatural realm, and therefore that there is no God. He also believed that physics is our best theory of the world; that is, physics is the final arbiter of truth.

- Because Quine believed that physics is true, and mathematics is the language of physics, mathematics must be true. But if mathematics is true, Quine argued, mathematical objects like numbers must exist.

- Quine—in line with Plato and most philosophers throughout history—believed that numbers and other mathematical objects are eternal and exist outside of space and time, outside of nature, outside of the realm of physics. Quine's naturalism led him to believe in a world outside of nature, a supernatural realm.

PART THREE

"Evil and Suffering Show There's No God"

19

YE OLDE PROBLEM OF EVIL

A DEFEATER FOR BELIEF IN GOD?

I t seems tolerably clear (to me, anyway) that science provides little to no evidence against God's existence—and if it provides any such evidence, it is wildly outweighed by the evidence that science provides *for* God's existence. And yet atheists claim that science in fact *shows* (a strong claim indeed) that God doesn't exist. They have wildly overstated their case. To those who have eyes to see, there is an overpowering appearance that the universe and its contents have been intricately designed.

But there is another powerful objection that confronts the religious believer, at least anyone who believes in a perfect, all-powerful, all-knowing God. In fact, this problem is seen to be powerful enough to nullify any evidence of design. In fact, it is seen as the strongest objection of all. Notice how Charles Darwin stated the problem in a letter to American botanist Asa Gray (who was an evangelical Presbyterian):

With respect to the theological view of the question; this is always painful to me. I am bewildered. I had no intention to write atheistically. But I own that I cannot see, as plainly as others do, and as I should wish to do, evidence of design and beneficence on all sides of us. There seems to me too much misery in the world. I cannot persuade myself that a beneficent and omnipotent God would have designedly created the Ichneumonidae [a type of wasp] with the express intention of their feeding within the living bodies of caterpillars, or that a cat should play with mice. Not believing this, I see no necessity in the belief that the eye was expressly designed.[1]

Why did Darwin have trouble seeing evidence of design as plainly as others do? It isn't because he didn't see the appearance of design. Indeed, the wasp's method of feeding its larvae is extremely clever. Rather it's that the cleverness looks *diabolical* rather than *divine*. This, to Darwin, seems somehow inconsistent with a "beneficent and omnipotent" God. But surely it isn't inconsistent with a designer of *some kind*. Yet that seems to be Darwin's conclusion. In other words, parts of nature, despite their cunning complexity, were so appalling to Darwin that he rejected design altogether. Better no designer than a demonic one.

This shows you how powerful the "problem of evil" is to many people. In fact, it is more than an intellectual problem; it is an emotional one, predicated on our natural and powerful revulsion to evil and suffering.

But what exactly *is* the problem here? Of course the existence of evil and suffering creates problems for humans—for example, the practical problem of avoiding and mitigating the evil that we and others experience. But that's not the problem in view here. The problem here is that a perfectly good, all-powerful, all-knowing God wouldn't allow the suffering of his creatures, and yet there *is* such suffering; therefore, there's no God.

My question is this: If you're a Christian, and someone presents this argument to you, do you now have evidence against God's existence? Or worse: Do you have evidence so powerful that you would be irrational to remain a believer? Do you have a defeater for your belief in God?

Not at all. But to see this, we need to slow down a bit, to look at the problem more carefully. What exactly is the substance of the atheist's claim? And, once we know what the claim is, is there any reason to believe it?

A SQUARE CIRCLE?

There are actually two different claims an atheist might make. The first, and traditional claim, is that there is a *logical* inconsistency between the existence of evil and the existence of a perfectly good, all-powerful, all-knowing God. There is, in other words, an outright logical contradiction between the propositions *God exists* and *Evil exists.* Both cannot possibly be true. As Hume put the problem: "Is God willing to prevent evil, but not able? Then he is impotent. Is he able but not willing? Then he is malevolent."[2] More recently, J. L. Mackie has said, regarding the "traditional problem of evil," "Here it can be shown, not merely that religious beliefs lack rational support, but that they are positively irrational, that the several parts of the essential theological doctrine are inconsistent with one another."[3] If evil exists, then God cannot be both all-powerful *and* all-good. And we couldn't object that God would stop evil if he knew about it. After all, God is also supposed to be *all*-knowing.

A God who allowed evil, then, would be like a square circle, so the claim goes. And not even God can create a square circle—or a married bachelor or a noncolored red object. Of course, that's not a mark against God—it's simply that these things aren't really *things* to be made; the words are meaningless. *God allows evil* is meaningless, logically incoherent. This is known as the "logical problem of evil."

So then, the existence of evil makes the existence of God impossible, not merely unlikely or improbable. If in fact there is a logical inconsistency between the existence of evil and God's existence, then everyone can go home. Game over. Nothing more to discuss. At least there's no God to be discussed. The atheist has a quick and clean victory.

PROBLEM SOLVED

But in the late 1960s and early '70s, Plantinga showed that there's no contradiction between God's existence and the existence of suffering. He was able to find a *logically possible* scenario in which evil and God coexist. That is, he showed that there is at least one possibility in which God is all-powerful, perfectly good, and all-knowing and allows evil. Plantinga didn't claim, however, that this is actually the way things are, although they could be. In other words, because the problem of evil made such a powerful claim—that God's existence is logically impossible given the evil we see—all Plantinga had to do was come up with a logically possible situation—even if it wasn't actual or even plausible. Because the problem was a purely logical one, the solution could be too.

Yet Plantinga's solution was plausible to boot.

His solution to this ancient problem hangs on the value of human freedom.[4] God wished his creatures to be capable of freely choosing— of their own accord—what is morally right. But this requires that they also be capable of freely choosing moral evil. So God couldn't forcibly prevent these creatures from choosing evil; if he did, they wouldn't choose freely. And, alas, these creatures did in fact use their freedom to choose evil, a choice that God could not have prevented while respecting their freedom. The nature of freedom and morality make it such that God could not prevent his creatures from making poor choices.

So, Plantinga argues—using some fairly sophisticated logical machinery—that, for all we know, God might not have been *able* to create free men who always do what is right, even though he's all-powerful. Again, the reason it's possible that God couldn't have done this has to do with the nature of freedom and the fact that no one can be forced to *freely* do something. The situation Plantinga describes is at least possible (although I think it is close to the sober truth). And this is all Plantinga needs to overcome the logical problem of evil. That is, "all" Plantinga had to do was show that it was *possible* that God be limited—or limit himself—in this way. In any case, in this story, the existence of evil is *our* fault, not God's. It was up to us to rebel against God and bring everything down with us. It was the *fall* after all. And if we were to be free, God couldn't stop us from falling.

Of course, saying that God can't do something causes the faithful to squirm; isn't it irreverent to say that God is limited in *any* way? But the Bible speaks of God's "inability" to do certain things—to lie, for example. And in the case of good and evil, God gave us the freedom to choose; simply by dint of freedom's nature, it was ultimately his own choice that limited him. He chose to let us freely choose.

Philosophers now concede that the traditional version of the problem of evil is entirely unsuccessful.[5] There is no *logical* inconsistency between God's existence and the existence of evil.

SWIMMING THE ATLANTIC?

But there is still much more for the believer to address. Just because it would be logically consistent that both God and evil existed, that, by itself, doesn't make it all that likely. Nothing about a human swimming the Atlantic, for example, violates the laws of logic; but it's improbable in the extreme. Atheists can still say (in fact they do say) that, given the existence of evil, it is so unlikely or improbable that God exists as to be wholly irrational to believe in him.[6]

This new "probabilistic" version of the argument—that it's unlikely or improbable that God exists—is not nearly as neat and clean as the logical problem of evil. Nor is it nearly as compelling. If it's logically possible that God could have allowed evil (which it seems

Plantinga has shown), then how might one show that it's *unlikely* that God exists?[7] Suppose that the atheist *could* do this. Suppose he could show that, given the truth of the proposition *Evil exists*, the probability of the truth of *God exists* is very low. That is, what if God's existence really were improbable given the fact that there is evil and suffering in the world?

By itself, this wouldn't show much. After all, there are many things that are improbable yet rational to believe.[8] Imagine you know that, years ago, you had a student who failed every math course he took, sometimes twice. Now, given what you know, the probability is very low that this student would go on to become a stellar engineering student, acing every mathematics course in graduate school. (This is in fact why colleges look at a student's transcripts.)

But then imagine you find out that, during his first year in college, he decided to get down to business and work diligently while also learning the proper study methods. You discover that all through high school this student was holding back, an under-achiever of the first order. Now, given *everything* you know, the probability of this student being an excellent engineering student is much higher.

So, even if the existence of evil—by itself—made it improbable that God exists, it could very well be that given everything you know, God's existence is still highly probable. For example, you may have some very good arguments for God's existence, arguments that entirely outweigh the existence of evil. Or perhaps the Holy Spirit has sufficiently repaired your *sensus divinitatis*, such that you just "see" that God exists—in fact, you *know* it. In either case, given everything you believe, it isn't improbable at all that God exists. In fact, given everything you believe, you *know* he does.

The atheist, to make the new probabilistic problem of evil plausible, will have to offer other arguments against God's existence, in addition to the probabilistic argument from evil.

This order is on the tall side.

SUFFERING FOR NO GOOD REASON

But I don't think it *is* improbable that God exists, even given just the fact of evil.[9] To argue that it's improbable that God would allow evil, the atheist would have to make a plausible case that God has no good reason for allowing evil. This new probabilistic version of the argument would have to go something like this: as far as we can tell, there's no good reason for God to permit evil, therefore it's highly unlikely that God exists.[10]

But why think that if we can't come up with a good reason for God permitting evil, that there isn't any reason? There are times when "absence of evidence is evidence of absence," but this doesn't seem to be one of them. Plantinga explains this with his "no-see-um" illustration.[11] Suppose, he says, that you look in your tent and don't see a St. Bernard. It would be entirely reasonable for you to believe that there's no St. Bernard in your tent. That's because if there were a St. Bernard in your tent, you would most likely see it. But now imagine that you look in your tent and, this time, you don't see any no-see-ums ("very small midges with a bite out of all proportion to their size"). What can you conclude? Perhaps there are no-see-ums in your tent; perhaps not. It's difficult to say. In either case, the inside of your tent would look the same. In the St. Bernard case, absence of evidence *is* evidence of absence. This is because I can expect to see a St. Bernard in my tent if there is one. But in the cases of no-see-ums (or bacteria or viruses), that same expectation would be entirely misguided.

And doesn't it seem like an explanation for why God permits evil is more like a no-see-um than a St. Bernard? After all, we're inquiring into whether *God* has a good reason. Now, the intellectual difference between God and humans isn't simply "really big," as if God merely has mental superpowers. The difference between our intellect and God's is infinite—God's intellect knows no bounds. This vast chasm is really not like an ordinary chasm at all; there is no approaching the other side. No matter how far you go across the chasm—suppose we have a bridge so we can continue the metaphor over the chasm—the other side is always beyond us. It seems plausible then to suppose that God has a good reason that we're simply not privy to right now—or perhaps ever. At least there seems no reason to think otherwise.

Look at it from a different angle. God's power and goodness are similarly infinite according to traditional Christian theology—and according to the atheist's argument as well. But if God is *that* kind of being, one powerful enough to eliminate all evil and suffering, couldn't his intellect be similarly vast, vast enough to have a good reason for permitting evil?[12]

The Bible is pretty clear about this.[13] When Job undergoes all manner of horrific suffering, he's perplexed, angry, and despondent. How could God do such a thing to him? After all, it's not as though Job is a tax collector or ax murderer. He's an upright fellow. And what was God's response to Job's complaints? Did God tell Job all the lofty reasons for letting him suffer? Not at all. Rather, God points out the vast difference between his and Job's understanding, quizzing Job on his penetrating insight into the depths of creation:

> Then the Lord spoke to Job out of the storm. He said: "Who is this that obscures my plans with words without knowledge? Brace yourself like a man; I will question you, and you shall answer me. Where were you when I laid the earth's foundation? Tell me, if you understand. Who marked off its dimensions? Surely you know! Who stretched a measuring line across it? On what were its footings set, or who laid its cornerstone—while the morning stars sang together and all the angels shouted for joy? . . . Surely you know, for you were already born! You have lived so many years!" (Job 38:1–7, 21)

Job takes God's ever-so-subtle hint, realizing that, in this case, the inference from "I don't know of any good reason for allowing this" to "There's *no* good reason for allowing this" is poor indeed. In a moment of perspective and clarity, Job responds, "Surely I spoke of things I did not understand, things too wonderful for me to know" (Job 42:3).

ANY SUGGESTIONS?

But isn't there *anything* we can say about why God permits so much evil and suffering? I think there is. We can at least gesture toward some reasons, as long as we keep in mind that we shouldn't expect them to solve all the intellectual difficulties. But perhaps just giving *some* sort of explanation might be enough to "hold us over" so to speak, until we know more or until the suffering is finally removed. Or both.

Tim Keller describes the responses he often receives after preaching on the story of Joseph. Recall that Joseph—a cocky, loudmouthed kid, to be sure—was treated miserably by his brothers. In a touching display of brotherly love, they sold Joseph into slavery. Things then went from bad to worse. Potiphar, Joseph's Egyptian master, put Joseph in prison (on the testimony of Potiphar's treacherous wife). He was now twice removed from freedom—slavery inside of slavery. But after Joseph's story is all told, we see that God used Joseph's suffering to bring about a greater good. Keller's point is that many people tell him that they find something similar in their own lives—that their greatest suffering turned out to be for their greatest good or the good of others. Not that they were happy about the suffering, but rather, they could see a possible point to it.[14]

We'll need to be careful, however. Keller's point isn't that we can see the actual purpose for most of the suffering in the world. We most definitely cannot. Rather, his point is that, if even *we* can see glimpses of reasons for *some* suffering, then it's reasonable to think that *God* would have good reasons for all suffering.

This doesn't answer all the serious puzzles that evil poses for the Christian. Even if God, in order to avoid making puppets pressed into loving him, had to create humans with free will and therefore with the distinct possibility of turning away from God, this doesn't explain the origin of our initial desire to rebel. Surely *God* didn't make us with that desire. Where then did it come from?

I don't know of anyone who has the answer to that question. But, again, perhaps we can gesture toward one. Perhaps, in God's creating beings in his image, with something of his nature, there is an inherent danger for these beings to be impressed with themselves. If so, then there would be the risk of these impressive creatures wishing to see themselves exalted. And perhaps this danger is extremely great. And perhaps, furthermore, the risk was well worth it, despite present appearances; after all, God had in mind a daring and costly plan to rescue our race in case that danger materialized.

RESCUED AT AN INFINITE COST

In fact, the plan's cost is a crucial part of understanding the Christian response to evil. Although atheist philosophers employ the problem of evil as an intellectual problem, much of the intellectual consternation is predicated on our natural revulsion to suffering and pain. The intellectual problem, it seems to me, is amplified by an emotional one.

And this is why the problem seems so compelling. After all, we've seen that the existence of evil isn't logically inconsistent with the existence of an all-powerful, perfectly good, all-knowing God. And the main reason to think that the existence of evil makes it unlikely that God exists, is that it would somehow be wrong for God to allow evil, that he ought not to allow it. In fact, many people, even if they don't think it's particularly unlikely that God would have a reason for allowing evil, find no consolation in that fact. Perhaps, they concede, God *does* have very good reasons for allowing evil. Nevertheless, they're still hurt, angry, and resentful, especially when the pain and suffering hit close to home.[15] When you or your loved ones undergo intense suffering, it can be difficult to see how any of the philosophical considerations matter.

This is where it is particularly useful to look more closely at the Christian story of redemption. God created humans to bless them, to allow them to enter a deep, fulfilling relationship with him. After all, our primary joys in life stem from our relationships with others; relationships are central to human flourishing, and a relationship with God himself *just is* human flourishing. It is the very thing we were made for. But in order to partake of this relationship, humans need to be like God in important ways—and so God made them in his likeness. Yet, as we saw, this move was rife with risk. Creatures made in God's image are intrinsically impressive, by dint of being so made.

There is, therefore, the temptation to be *too* impressed. It is perfectly right for God to be the object of worship and adoration. Indeed, it would be morally wrong for him not to be, and wrong for him not to want it. But it is entirely different for us; to put oneself above the most perfect being is morally wrong. Yet this, apparently, is what we desired. We wanted things that only God could have. And in trying to take them, we marred our very natures, so that—although we still retain something of God's image—it is badly misshapen. And now, of course, we're suffering for it.

But God has suffered more. Infinitely more, in fact. The key to understanding this is God's triune nature, the Trinity. Because God exists as three persons, there is an extremely close relationship between the Father, the Son, and the Holy Spirit. These three persons are infinitely close, having been in this relationship for all of eternity. In fact, this relationship is the central reality. What's more is that God has graciously invited us into this relationship, a relationship that would make us entirely complete.

When God's Son was crucified some two thousand years ago by the Roman government, the eternal relationship between the Father and Son was severed. This is why the cross is so horrific. To be sure, the physical suffering was genuine suffering, but that suffering was negligible compared to the pain of losing this infinitely close relationship. Anyone who has felt the pain of a lost relationship—especially a close one—knows that this suffering can be devastating. Separation from someone you love is nearly unbearable. And in Jesus' case, the pain would be infinite.

God, then, suffered an excruciating evil, and on our behalf.[16] This is no small thing, and it may be of some comfort. Realizing that God himself suffered far greater pain to save creatures who—at the time of their rescue—hated him, might offer some perspective.

Notice, too, that this sort of consideration is something that is available only to Christians, to those who believe in a triune God.[17] And, Plantinga reminds us, "in being offered eternal fellowship with God, we human beings are invited to join the charmed circle of the trinity itself."[18] And so, "perhaps that invitation can be issued only to creatures who have fallen, suffered, and been redeemed. If so, the condition of humankind is vastly better than it would have been, had there been no sin and no suffering. *O Felix Culpa*, indeed!"[19] *O Felix Culpa*: "O Happy Fall!" Ironic, paradoxical, yet a story with a wildly happy ending. But like all riveting stories, the journey is at times unbearable.

The problem of evil, while still a problem for the believer, isn't one that makes belief in God irrational. And so despite the problem's centrality in the atheist's arsenal, it is surprisingly weak, from an intellectual standpoint. But there is more to say about evil, this time about its implications for the atheist or, more accurately, naturalism's implication for morality in general. And the conclusion is simplicity itself: if there is no God, there is no evil.

Nor is there any good.

FOR YOUR ARSENAL

- There are two versions of the problem of evil, the logical problem and the probabilistic problem.

- In the case of the logical problem of evil, the existence of God and the existence of evil allegedly result in a full-blown logical contradiction. This problem was solved by showing that there is a logically possible situation in which God and evil exist simultaneously. In particular, it is possible that God couldn't make free creatures who refrain from evil.

- In the case of the probabilistic problem of evil, the existence of evil makes it *highly unlikely* (but not impossible) that God exists. After all, we can't think of any good reason that he would allow evil. But even though *we* can't think of a reason, for all we know, God has very good ones.

20

THE ATHEIST'S PROBLEM

{OF EVIL}

BELIEVERS HAVE DONE SOME
REALLY BAD THINGS

The careful reader will have gleaned that atheists have a problem with religion; namely, they think that it's irrational. At best, atheists believe that the Christian suffers from a particularly nasty form of cognitive malfunction. This should, one would think, prompt a deep sense of pity and compassion toward the typical religious believer. Those who believe in God are intellectually deformed, and this is indeed a tragedy.

But this isn't usually the atheist's response. Rather, many contemporary atheists respond with anger and disgust, as if the religious believer is somehow morally culpable for her belief in God. One of the common threads running throughout contemporary atheists' writings is a highly developed sense of moral rage. We saw that Dawkins believes that religious education is worse than sexual abuse and that children should therefore be protected from their religious parents and teachers. Daniel Dennett believes that "safety demands that religions be put in cages," if they get out of hand.[1] To be sure, we should try to preserve religious folk, just as we should try to preserve dangerous beasts in zoos:

> Save the Baptists! Yes, of course, but not *by all means*. Not if it means tolerating the deliberate misinforming of children about the natural world. According to a recent poll, 48 percent of the people in the United States today believe that the book of Genesis is literally true. . . . Misinforming a child is a terrible offense.[2]

And what is more common than traipsing out the immense horrors committed in the name of religion? Religion, as Christopher Hitchens says, poisons everything.[3] Although he's paid this compliment to all religions, he has famously called Christianity a "wicked cult."[4] Not merely a tragically misinformed cult or a somewhat naughty cult, but one that is downright wicked.

Of course, charges of religious hypocrisy are one of the more delicious attacks on Christians. And for good reason too: there is plenty of evidence for such hypocrisy. What is more common than Charlie Church over there in the next cubicle surfing the web during business hours immediately after chiding you for using your favorite four-letter word?

And then there are the countless religious wars and the violence committed in God's name. From the Inquisitions (Spanish and Roman) and the Thirty Years' War, to "Belfast, Beirut, Bombay, Belgrade, Bethlehem, and Baghdad," which Hitchens points out are just those in the *B*s.[5]

There is no getting around the fact that all these examples (and many more besides) are a blight on humanity. Neither is there any need to try getting around it. For one thing, we're quite aware that religious folk have for centuries tried to corner the market on violence and wickedness. But—and here's the flip side—they just cant seem to succeed. In *The Devil's Delusion*, David Berlinski somberly lists the number of deaths in the twentieth century's wars, a total in untold millions, far more than anything seen or imagined previously. And most of these wars have been conducted by extremely serious atheists, atheists who have taken blind evolution just as seriously. It's fairly obvious that it was the implications of atheism, with its lack of restraint (more on this in a moment), that have led to far more suffering than anything religion has devised.

Of course, atheists can get rather prickly when we make this sort of claim.[6] And suppose it isn't true at all, and that both sides are pretty even in their success at causing human misery, or that religion actually won the dubious distinction. Would that show that religion per se is wicked or that those who believe in God are—by that fact alone—deserving of moral condemnation?

It is difficult to see how. After all, if we were looking "scientifically" at the situation, attempting to determine what causes killing, torturing, raping, and other similar activities, we might conclude—at least it's plausible to conclude—that the cause is always one or more humans. After all, in each and every one of those activities we find humans committing the act. Some of these are folks who believe in God; others aren't. It appears that a common factor is mankind, not religion. Just a thought.

"BAD QUARK!"

That's not to say that belief (or disbelief) in God makes no difference. For example, it's plausible that a worldview according to which humans are ultimately (and only) collections of particles, accidently put together, would tend to suggest that there are no moral actions whatsoever. I'll let Dawkins explain:

> Think about it. On one planet, and possibly only one planet in the
> entire universe, molecules that would normally make nothing more

complicated than a chunk of rock, gather themselves together into chunks of rock-sized matter of such staggering complexity that they are capable of running, jumping, swimming, flying, seeing, hearing, capturing and eating other such animated chunks of complexity; capable in some cases of thinking and feeling, and falling in love with yet other chunks of complex matter.[7]

Putting it in terms of mere chunks of matter gives the issue a certain clarity. Some of these chunks of matter—humans—seem to perform actions of hatred and cruelty, love and compassion; and most of these actions seem either morally right or morally wrong. But are they really? We don't, for example, think that the rock (or piano) that fell on you and killed you is morally culpable (although we would no doubt be distraught). Neither do we typically think that cancer is morally blameworthy for someone's death. Why then think that more complicated chunks like us, made of the same stuff (quarks or whatever), would be morally blameworthy?

It is difficult to see how an ultimately impersonal world of nothing but atoms could have anything like morality, and there are currently no good reasons to think otherwise. At least not an absolute morality, one that is person-independent and therefore not subject to the whims of human likes, dislikes, desires, loves, and fears.

Suppose that morals are merely dependent on what we think and feel. Such morals shouldn't be at all compelling. And at the very least, morality shouldn't be as compelling as we currently believe it to be. After all, atheists often point out that different cultures can have different systems of morality. My guess is that the ethical disparity between cultures is not as large as is sometimes claimed. Nevertheless, there are cultures—"Nazi culture" is always a good example—in which the ethical norm or standard has some highly questionable aspects to it. But if humans are the ultimate standard, then who's to say what's questionable? Humans are free to choose, each of them for themselves. Morality looks to be a matter of taste. "Evil" becomes "I don't like it" or "Not cool."

YOU BE THE JUDGE

Now, if humans are the product of blind evolution, an absence of absolute moral standards looks extremely plausible. According to the Grand Evolutionary Myth, our moral beliefs have evolved right along with our heads, shoulders, knees, and toes. In "Morality without Religion" biologist Marc Hauser and philosopher Peter Singer write: "Our evolved [moral] intuitions do not necessarily give us the right or consistent answers to moral dilemmas. What was good for our ancestors may not be good for human beings as a whole today, let alone for our planet and all the other beings living on it."[8] They go on to make the entirely reasonable inference—given the standard evolutionary story—that

> in this respect, it is important for us to be aware of the universal set of moral intuitions so that we can reflect on them and, if we choose, to act contrary to them. We can do this without blasphemy, because it is our own nature, not God, that is the source of our species morality.[9]

Similarly, Sam Harris says, "We are the final judges of what is good. . . ."[10] So, we can decide, if we like, to change the rules. And of course, since there is no higher authority to which we must answer, such changes are perfectly legitimate. In fact, the rest of Harris's sentence continues, ". . . just as we remain the final judges of what is logical." We can bend the rules, and even break them. In the end, *we* set the standards. Don't tell my logic students.

Of course, we're still evolving according to the Grand Evolutionary Myth. Evolution is "interested" in survival; this is what it "selects" for. But scientists have pointed out that the goal of survival doesn't always lead to the moral intuitions we currently prefer. According to philosopher of science Samir Okasha, sociobiologists argue that behavior such as "rape, aggression, xenophobia, and male promiscuity" give the human organism a survival advantage. And, he continues, "In each case, their argument is the same: individuals who engage in the behaviour out-reproduced individuals who didn't, and the behaviour was genetically based, hence transmitted from parents to their offspring."[11]

If the sociobiologists' argument is at all on the right track, and given blind evolution, then our current ethical beliefs—that rape, aggression, and so forth are morally wrong—are at odds with what accords with evolution.

But, some people object, the sociobiologists' argument could excuse the rapist as merely doing what is "natural," that it's just part of his genetics. But, says Okasha, the truth isn't always pleasant: "Ethics cannot be deduced from science. So there is nothing ideologically suspect about sociobiology. Like all sciences, it is simply trying to tell us the facts about the world. Sometimes the facts are disturbing, but we must learn to live with them."[12] And many people who believe in unguided evolution are convinced that—to echo Ingrid Newkirk, cofounder of PETA—"a rat is a pig is a dog is a boy."[13] And, she might have added, is a cockroach is a squash is a rock.

Okasha also points out the important fact/value distinction. It's one thing to describe the *facts* of a situation; it's quite another to describe what a person *ought* to do. But Stenger claims that "even the principles of morality are subject to scientific investigation since they involve observable human behavior."[14] Stenger is mistaken here. Science can study what humans *do*, but not what they *ought* to do. A moral standard, a yardstick for measuring right and wrong, good and evil, is something quite different from the thing being measured. And it's not as if we can find the measuring stick if we stare long and hard enough at the thing being measured. Hume made a similar point when he argued that we can't derive an "ought" from an "is."

Fundamental to morality is the notion that there is a way that humans ought (and ought not) to act. But what would it take for humans to be under such an obligation? To whom are they obligated? To put the question slightly differently, Dawkins asks, "If we reject Deuteronomy and Leviticus (as all enlightened moderns must do), by what criteria do we then decide which of religion's moral values to *accept*?"[15] He's got a point; it's a good question.

MY SOLIDARITY OR YOURS?

Perhaps we passed over too quickly the idea that *we* are the standard, that humans are what grounds morality and that this grounding is enough to give us a robust ethical system. Perhaps our ultimate obligation is to other humans; perhaps it is our being part of a common humanity, a global family, that creates obligations, each to all. And perhaps this is what Christopher Hitchens meant when he recently wrote, "It is our innate solidarity, and not some despotism of the sky, which is the source of our morality and our sense of decency."[16] It's not entirely clear what "solidarity" amounts to for Hitchens. Perhaps he means that, as Sam Harris says in a similar context, "We are bound to one another."[17] It's a touching sentiment.

Is our solidarity, our "oneness," enough to generate obligations strong enough to give us the morality we've become accustomed to? Suppose two people disagree about what obligations humans generally have. Can one of them be right? If so, by what standard? What shall we use as the moral yardstick? Surely it can't be what the "majority" of humans think. After all, what the majority thinks can change over time. And it is fairly clear that atheists wouldn't like this democratic process of choosing morality: most humans today probably disagree with them on a number of important ethical issues. And if the Nazis (them again) had won the Second World War, we'd have a different set of *legitimate and binding* ethical standards. A different set of oughts. At least if mere solidarity is the source of morality.

Also, suppose Hitchens and I disagree about some matter of morality. Suppose I tell him he should conform to my ethical standards. Suppose he disagrees. Why should he not simply tell me—with all due respect—to shove it?

Recall that atheists like Hitchens are calling for a new Enlightenment. Remember, too, that the motto of the Enlightenment was "Have courage to use your own understanding!" The Enlightenment, if it was anything, was a call to reject tradition, testimony, and the dreaded herd mentality. We can hear the echoes of this in Stenger's heroic pronouncement: "[Atheists] rely on their own consciences and not what someone else tells them is right or wrong."[18] Listening to my own conscience and disregarding what others tell me to do is apparently encouraged by these atheists. Unless, of course, the "others" are atheists.

And so the notion of "solidarity" seems to be rather at odds with the atheists' coming Enlightenment. After all, what if I come to the conclusion—even after long and honest consideration—that I'm simply not interested in solidarity? Would that be wrong? Says who? I'm using my own understanding. Why would you—as an Enlightenment lover—ask me to use *yours*?

BEDROCK

Humans can't be the standard of absolute right and wrong. If there is one thing I'm confident of, it's that—regardless of what anyone thinks—rape is wrong in an objective and absolute sense. And it wouldn't do any good to argue the point. After all, any premises used in such an argument would be no stronger than my belief that rape is wrong. I'm as confident about this belief as I am about any of my beliefs. And, thankfully, nearly all of us—theists and atheists alike—agree that rape is very wrong. We believe this even if, as sociobiologists claim, rape provided some sort of survival advantage. If faced with a choice, we'd all rather forgo survival.

Why do we all generally agree? Has evolution helpfully winnowed out those who would have otherwise disagreed with us? Did they win the Darwin Award by being eliminated from the gene pool, allowing *our* morality to be the "correct" morality? Whatever the case, it is generally agreed that those of us here have a cognitive faculty that delivers fairly uniform moral views. Hauser and Singer point to studies that "prove empirical support for the idea that like other psychological faculties of the mind, including language and mathematics, we are endowed with a moral faculty that guides our intuitive judgments of right and wrong."[19] And even Hitchens noted that "the so-called

Golden Rule is innate in us, or is innate except in the sociopaths who do not care about others, and the psychopaths who take pleasure in cruelty."[20]

It is, I think, quite true that we have a moral cognitive faculty, that our judgments of morality are (in large part) innate. In fact, we saw that the Scriptures seem to indicate as much, that the moral law is written on our hearts. Even on the hearts of Gentiles.

And now we're back to an important question. What is the origin of this cognitive faculty? Why think that it's reliable? What are its credentials? We saw the importance of origins in an earlier chapter. Plantinga argued that if we were completely at a loss about our origins (as Hume claimed to be), then we have very little reason to think that our cognitive faculties are generally reliable. Similarly, we saw that if we believe our origins were accidental, as in the Grand Evolutionary Myth, we still have reason not to trust our cognitive faculties. And so, on the evolutionary story, we would have reason to mistrust our moral cognitive faculty. After all, if blind evolution is the source, then rape and incest are adaptive for survival, as sociobiologists tell us. And yet these are clearly and extremely wrong, if anything is. Blind evolution gives the wrong answers. It seems that we are more certain about the wickedness of these actions than we are about the theory of blind evolution. But the former tells against the latter.

SURVIVAL VERSUS OUGHT

But suppose blind evolution can account for all our strongly held moral judgments. That is, suppose we can see how *all* our moral views give us a survival advantage. (Let us assume also that there is 100 percent agreement between us on our moral judgments.) Suppose we agree with Victor Stenger that "it is very easy to give nonsupernatural reasons for preferring honesty to lying, for outlawing murder to theft. . . . So whatever useful moral prescriptions religion has provided are equally available without it."[21]

We think lying is wrong because societies in which liars run rampant soon run out of time; similarly for incest, a practice that tends to result in fewer viable offspring. Even if our current ethical standards agreed with the predicted results of standard evolutionary theory, our ethical obligations would still not be in any way binding. In other words, although blind evolution—on our generous supposition—accounts for our moral *beliefs*, it still doesn't account for genuine moral *reality*. There's still no ought. We may believe that torturing kittens is wrong, but that, by itself, wouldn't imply that we ought to refrain from it. Our moral preference or taste is an evolutionary accident.

But again, if I'm confident of anything—and no doubt you feel the same—I'm confident that it would be wrong to torture kittens *regardless of what anyone thinks*. In a universe in which everyone thought that torturing kittens is a fine idea, one indicative of moral excellence, it would still be wrong to torture kittens. Again, I have no argument for this, since any premise would be no stronger than the conclusion.

Behavior is either right or wrong, regardless of what we think, or else it isn't genuinely right or wrong, at least not in any objective or absolute sense, a sense in which morality isn't merely dependent upon what we believe.

So the status of morality seems to depend, in part at least, on the origins of the universe and how the whole cosmic establishment is run. In particular, if we're here because of blind evolution, then as Dawkins points out, there is "at bottom, no design," and so there is "no purpose, no evil, no good, nothing but pitiless indifference."[22] And he's absolutely right. A world of pure accident, with no one running the joint, has no rules. It's as impersonal as a rock—a chunk of quarks.

REPLACING THE OLD PROBLEM OF EVIL WITH A NEW ONE

The traditional Christian response to all this is that there could be no moral obligation unless there is a divine lawgiver. If we are to have genuine morality, the universe must be fundamentally personal, run by a personal being to whom we are obligated, one whose nature is such that rape is wrong and loving one's neighbor is good.[23]

Now suppose you believe that there *is* such a thing as evil. Suppose further you believe that the existence of evil requires a divine lawgiver who can underwrite our absolute obligations. If so, Plantinga points out, you have an argument *for* God's existence, an argument from the existence of evil.[24] In fact, the existence of morality in general—good *and* evil—will provide strong evidence for a divine lawgiver. Of course, this argument is only as strong as your belief that there is genuine good and evil. It's only as strong as your belief, for example, that pedophilia is objectively wrong—wicked in an absolute sense. But, I daresay, you have few beliefs that you hold more strongly.

Also notice that if there's no evil, then, in some sense there's no traditional problem of evil. That is, the atheist's argument required that there be moral evil; after all it is the existence of evil that is inconsistent with God's existence. Without evil, however, the argument simply doesn't work. This realization—perhaps combined with that of the previous paragraph—is what drew C. S. Lewis away from atheism. In *Mere Christianity* he wrote,

> My argument against God was that the universe seemed so cruel and unjust. But how had I got this idea of *just* and *unjust?* . . . Of course I could have given up my idea of justice by saying it was nothing but a private idea of my own. But if I did that, then my argument against God collapsed too—for the argument depended on saying that the world was really unjust, not simply that it did not happen to please my private fancies.[25]

Again, if you don't think there *is* such a thing as justice or injustice (apart from our own "private fancies"), then this won't apply to you—you won't be pressured (at least by this) to concede that God exists. But you'll have another, more pressing problem, a new problem of evil. As

Hitchens said, "A person who thought that heaven and hell were empty could conclude that he was free to do exactly as he wished."[26]

Not only could that person conclude this, but that person *ought* to.

And in such a case, everything becomes permissible. And that's a problem indeed.

CAN ATHEISTS BEHAVE WELL?

The atheist is not without a reply, of course. Hitchens:

> Exchange views with a believer even for a short time. . . . It will not be long until you are politely asked how you can possibly know right from wrong. Without holy awe, what is to prevent you from resorting to theft, murder, rape, and perjury? It will sometimes be conceded that non-believers have led ethical lives, and it will also be conceded (as it had better be) that many believers have been responsible for terrible crimes. Nonetheless, the working assumption is that we should have no moral compass if we were not somehow in thrall to an unalterable and unchallengeable celestial dictatorship. What a repulsive idea![27]

Much of what Hitchens said here is certainly correct. He was absolutely right that atheists can behave at least as well as believers, indeed much better sometimes. Furthermore, Hitchens was right that the reason many people behave well is because they *believe* it's good to do so, because of a natural feeling of revulsion toward certain types of behavior and a concomitant feeling of guilt whenever they act a certain way. People don't necessarily love their neighbor because they're afraid of divine punishment (although that can certainly play a role, and sometimes quite appropriately). And we've seen that there is some behavior we consider morally wrong that is also detrimental to an organism's survival. On all these things, Hitchens couldn't have been more right.

But all of that is entirely beside the point. The real point isn't whether atheists can behave well; of course they can. Nor is it whether they *want* to behave well; thankfully they do. Rather, the point is whether atheists can say why they *ought* to behave well. And I mean a moral ought. To be sure, atheists can say that *if* humans want a better chance at survival, then they *ought* to refrain from lying, raping, incest, and so on. But that pragmatic kind of ought isn't the one in view here. Rather, we're asking whether it is simply and fundamentally right to refrain from these behaviors and genuinely wrong to perform them, regardless of whether it is convenient or beneficial for one's health or general well-being. Is morality an objective—a human independent—part of the cosmos?

If it isn't, God help us.

CAN GOD BE THE STANDARD?

But there is another common objection, this one going back at least to Plato's dialogue the *Euthyphro*, and so it's called the "Euthyphro objection." Stenger puts it this way: "Either God defines what is good, in which case it is arbitrary, or God is inherently good, in which case goodness is defined independent of God."[28] In other words, if good is simply "what God commands," then he could conceivably command rape, in which case rape would be good. On the other hand, if God commands things *because* they're good, there must be some standard external to God that defines good and evil. That is, God has to check with the standard before issuing a command.

Well, which is it? According to traditional Christian theology, there's nothing outside God with which he must confer, nothing that tells him whether an action is in the right or wrong column. Instead, that which makes something good or bad is God himself. And therefore, if God were to command rape, say, then that would be, by definition, good. But, traditionally, God is a *necessary* being: he has to exist, in the same way a bachelor must be unmarried. Furthermore,

God's character is necessary as well. That is, just as God cannot lie, neither can he command rape. Therefore, the "If God commanded rape" part of the choice could never be satisfied.[29] It would be similar to saying "If God made a square circle then . . ."

So then, the moral standard is God's own character, a character that cannot be otherwise. This is where we reach the ground floor. Again, as Wittgenstein said, explanations must eventually come to an end. And in every case, the explanation, according to Christianity, stops at God. And that seems like a good place to stop.

FOR YOUR ARSENAL

- If there is no absolute divine lawgiver, then humans have no absolute obligations that underwrite an absolute moral standard.

- Science cannot show how we ought to behave. Describing what we do doesn't tell us what we ought to do.

- God's unchangeable character is the standard of good and evil. Because his character could not possibly be different (it is necessarily the way it is) the moral standards are absolute and cannot possibly be different from what they are.

21

CONCLUSION: DAMAGED GOODS

Three concepts have risen to the surface during our discussion, each corresponding to one of the book's three parts: *rationality, design,* and *absolute standards.* Rationality was the main concept in Part 1, where we addressed the charge that belief in God isn't rational because it lacks adequate evidence. In Part 2 we saw that science, rather than showing that God doesn't exist, provides powerful evidence for divine design. The conclusion of the final section, Part 3, was that, in order to have an objective human independent morality, we need an absolute moral standard, one underwritten by an absolute lawgiver. These three notions—rationality, design, and absolute standards—are brought together in an unexpected way, in a single concept that cuts deeply across the entire discussion. This connection—the concept of *proper function*—gives us good reason to think that atheism is undone.

RATIONALITY, DESIGN, AND
PROPER FUNCTION

There were hints of this from the very beginning. Remember, we're rational when we believe on the basis of *properly functioning* cognitive faculties. Now, when something is functioning properly—a car, say—it is functioning as it should, as it ought. In other words, it is functioning as it was intended. The intentions here are those of the designer(s). A car functions properly when it's operating as it was designed to. And when we say that a car is *mal*functioning—when the master cylinder needs replacing and the brakes go all the way to the floor—we're saying that it's *not* working the way it's supposed to, the way it was designed to.

This notion of proper function (and dysfunction)—as we've applied it to the car—depends essentially on the notion of design. And, going out on a limb, if something is designed, there's a designer. Designing is an intentional act, one requiring a person, human or divine.

Of course, in the case of a car, we're talking about something *obviously* designed. But in the case of rationality, we're applying the notion of proper function to *us*, or to parts of us, at least.[1] Is this application legitimate?

Well, even in the ordinary business of life, we apply the notion of proper function to organisms, human or otherwise. In fact, this use is crucial to medicine, biology, and other sciences. When we suffer from a high level of creatinine in our blood, it's a sign that our kidneys are not functioning properly. The eyes of someone born blind aren't working as they should, as they ought. So, the application of dysfunction and proper function to organisms is something the scientific field does all the time. Hopefully it's legitimate. In any case, it's unavoidable.

Such talk, however, seems to imply that humans have a design, and so seems to imply the existence of a designer. But does it really? After all, you don't have to believe in God to see when someone is sick and not functioning as she should.[2] Anyone can see that. So does such talk really imply that the person is designed?

Well, true enough: anyone *can* see that a person is suffering from a disease and therefore not functioning properly. The real question, however, is whether the atheist can make sense of this inevitable way of looking at the world.

In *Warrant and Proper Function*, Plantinga canvasses a number of the most plausible "designer-free" explanations of proper function and shows them all seriously defective. For example, when we say that a horse isn't functioning properly, we don't mean that it's not functioning like a normal or ordinary horse. This is the statistical sense of "normal." Proper function and dysfunction can't be explained in terms of what is normal, because even a normal organism may function improperly. For example, suppose most sixty-year-old carpenters have lost a finger; that is, it's normal for older carpenters to have no more than nine fingers.[3] But we wouldn't then say that a sixty-year-old carpenter with all ten fingers is malfunctioning. Similarly, we wouldn't say that a horse that could run 10 percent faster than any other horse was functioning improperly. Proper function can't be founded on statistical normalcy. There are many cases where these concepts come apart.

Let's return to rationality. The problem with the notion of rationality—the problem for atheists anyway—is that it requires the notion of proper function, which, in turns, seems to depend on the notion of design. That is, asking whether or not something—be it artifact or organism—is functioning properly is the same as asking whether it is functioning according to a designer's plan.

In any case, atheists have yet to come up with a purely naturalistic account of proper function. And the prospects look dim.

PROPER FUNCTION AND ABSOLUTE STANDARDS

Now, notice that the designer's intentions are a standard by which we measure the organism or artifact. Does the organism's function meet the designer's standards? Is the organism or artifact functioning as it ought? Just as we compare a length of rope to a length of measuring tape, we are comparing the function of the object to the designer's standard.

So we have connected rationality to proper function, and proper function to a standard. Now, whether or not a horse or human is suffering from a form of dysfunction isn't up to us. Either your kidneys are malfunctioning or they are not. Time will tell, regardless of what *we* say. It seems then that if we're to have genuine proper function (and genuine dysfunction)—at least in the absolute sense to which we're accustomed—we need a standard that's independent of us. And this is just what we saw when it came to an absolute moral standard. We need a human-independent standard of morality if rape and torture are genuinely wrong. An "ought" needs a person, and the absolute "oughts" require an absolute personal being. And that's something a purely naturalistic world can't give us.

So there's a problem of evil for atheists, as we saw, namely, whether they can hit upon an all-natural explanation for evil (and morality in general). There are similar problems for other concepts that require absolute standards; there's a problem of good and a problem of proper function. Therefore, there's also a problem of rationality and of logic. All of these require absolute standards, and so they're all problems for the atheist, someone who believes that the world is accidental, impersonal, and without design.

Consider logic. An application of one of the fundamental rules of logic is that an object cannot be both red and not-red at the same time and in the same sense. Now, recall that Sam Harris said, "We are the final judges of what is good, just as we remain the final judges of what is logical."[4] But is it really up to us as to whether an object can be both red and non-red at the same time and in the same sense?

ATHEISM IS A FORM OF COGNITIVE DYSFUNCTION

So then, our three sections all come together here at the end. If what we've said throughout is anywhere close to being true, then the notions of *design, rationality,* and *absolute standards* cannot exist in a naturalistic world, in the world of the atheists. Without absolute standards—of which there must be many—their worldview would entirely collapse.

And this poses a serious problem for any atheist who claims that belief in God is irrational. In fact, it takes the legs right out from under such a claim. If there is no designer, then there is no proper function, and therefore there is no such thing as irrationality. But then there's no such thing as rationality either. There's only a sterile, impersonal "desert landscape." Beliefs are neither rational nor irrational. They just are.[5]

But if the Christian story is true, then there *is* such a thing as irrationality. And as we saw, those who don't believe in God are suffering from it. After all, unbelief is caused, in part, by the malfunctioning of the *sensus divinitatis.* Originally, this natural cognitive mechanism would cause us to believe in God as naturally as you believe in ordinary material objects. Yet our tragic and treacherous rebellion against the Lord, in an extreme case of self-aggrandizement, resulted in serious cognitive malfunction. That is, our natural cognitive faculty that would have naturally caused us to believe in God no longer functions as it ought, no longer works according to design. And this is the very definition of irrationality.

So, either there's no proper (or improper) function, or else the atheist has cognitively malfunctioned. To put it a bit differently, either there's no such thing as rationality (or irrationality) or else atheism is irrational. But atheists will heartily agree that there *is* such a thing as irrationality; they point to *us* as examples of it. In any case, that leaves only one option: atheists are damaged goods.

Of course, all of us are damaged goods. Sin has caused some degree of irrationality in us all. And given the extent of the damage, it's no wonder atheists don't believe. The real wonder is why *anyone* believes. The explanation, of course, is that God has begun to repair humanity, at an unimaginable cost to himself.

And this is really good news.

FOR YOUR ARSENAL

- There are three concepts—rationality, design, and absolute standards—associated with the three parts of the book, respectively. All are connected through the notion of proper function.

- A *rational* belief is one that is formed by a cognitive faculty that is *functioning properly* (in the appropriate environment). The proper function of something depends on how it was intended to function, on what it was *designed* to do. The design is the *standard* by which we measure whether something is functioning properly.

- There is currently no natural way to account for our notion of proper function. If something can function properly or improperly apart from our opinions, then there must be a human-independent standard of proper function. There must also be, therefore, a human-independent design.

- Rationality and irrationality require a divine designer. So if the atheist is right, and there's no divine designer, then there's no such thing as rationality (or irrationality, and so belief in God *isn't* irrational). If the atheist is wrong, on the other hand, and there *is* a divine designer, then the atheist is irrational (because of the malfunction of the *sensus divinitatis*).

- The solution to mankind's innate insanity, insanity caused by the malfunctioning of the *sensus divinitatis*, is the restoration that comes by embracing the gospel of Jesus Christ.

ACKNOWLEDGMENTS

The general idea for this book was largely Joel Miller's, the Vice President of Acquisitions and Editorial at Thomas Nelson's Nonfiction Trade Group. For the opportunity he provided, and his encouragement throughout, I am extremely grateful. Among other things, writing this book has allowed me to consolidate many of my percolating thoughts on these topics. More importantly, writing a book like this was the reason I left engineering for philosophy in the first place.

We hatched the project over a working lunch and although its final shape is somewhat different from what we initially discussed, the book's intent is, I trust, the same: to address the recent avalanche of writings by belligerent atheists—atheists with ridiculously unwarranted confidence in the strength of their arguments. Additionally, the book still intends to boost the confidence of believers, particularly those who have been misled to believe that these militant atheists are at least writing in good faith, that they really have reason to sound so darn confident.

Joel turned out to be one of my editors as well, giving me insightful advice without trying to exercise excessive control. My guess is that he's a good dad.

Others at Thomas Nelson have also made this book much better than it otherwise would have been: Janene MacIvor, my other editor, and those who work for her, kept me on the straight and narrow, exhibiting eagle-eyes and a dexterity for guiding the book through the circuitous path to publication.

Many of the ideas in this book are, naturally enough, not my own. I'm indebted to a host of thinkers far more capable than I, those who, over the last decade or so, have revolutionized my thinking on these topics, just as they have for many others in the philosophy world. But there are three philosophers in particular whom I wish to acknowledge here: Alvin Plantinga, Nicholas Wolterstorff, and Peter van Inwagen. I had the privilege of seeing these men—up close and in real life—do what they do best. Each of them is a paragon of philosophical acumen—and all three are devout Christians (someday this won't be a qualification that needs mentioning). In fact, another *raison d'être* for this book is to familiarize more people outside philosophy with their work. I offer them great thanks.

The book's main title was really N.D. Wilson's brainchild. Nate is always good for ideas that are simultaneously creative and subversive. The title's multi-layered meaning was an instant and lasting hit with me.

My agent, Aaron Rench, is the crucial link between me and the greater world. He never ceases to amaze me with what seems like otherworldly magic.

Finally, thanks goes to Christine, my wife,—for innumerable things, of course—but here I refer to the fact that nothing I write reaches public consumption without going through her first. And when it does, she's its most enthusiastic supporter.

NOTES

Introduction

1. Sam Harris, *The End of Faith: Religion, Terror, and the Future of Reason* (New York: W. W. Norton & Company, 2004), 72.
2. Victor J. Stenger, *The New Atheism: Taking a Stand for Science and Reason* (Ahmherst, NY: Prometheus Books, 2009), 15.
3. Christopher Hitchens, ed., *The Portable Atheist: Essential Readings for the Nonbeliever* (Cambridge, MA: Da Capo Press, 2007), xi.
4. Richard Dawkins, *The God Delusion* (Boston: Houghton Mifflin Company, 2006), 127.
5. Daniel C. Dennett, "The Bright Stuff," *The New York Times*, July 12, 2003, accessed February 6, 2012, http://www.nytimes.com/2003/07/12/opinion/the-bright-stuff.html.
6. Dawkins, *The God Delusion*, 380.
7. Christopher Hitchens, *God Is Not Great: How Religion Poisons Everything* (New York: Twelve, 2007), 5.
8. David Berlinski, *The Devil's Delusion: Atheism and Its Scientific Pretensions* (New York: Crown Forum, 2008), 6.
9. Harris, *The End of Faith: Religion, Terror, and the Future of Reason*, 48.
10. Nicholas Humphrey, http://www.humphrey.org.uk/papers/1998WhatShallWeTell.pdf. Quoted in Peter Hitchens, *The Rage against God: How Atheism Led Me to Faith* (Grand Rapids, MI: Zondervan, 2010), 207–8.
11. Dawkins, *The God Delusion*, 356.
12. Hitchens, *The Rage against God: How Atheism Led Me to Faith*, 173–74.

13. Hitchens, *God Is Not Great: How Religion Poisons Everything*, 283.

14. Christopher Hitchens and Douglas Wilson, *Is Christianity Good for the World?* (Moscow, ID: Canon Press, 2008), 11.

15. "Religion: Modernizing the Case for God," *TIME* online, April 7, 1980, accessed February 6, 2012, http://www.time.com/time/ magazine/article/0,9171,921990,00.html.

16. Alvin Plantinga, "Reason and Belief in God," in *Faith and Rationality: Reason and Belief in God*, ed. Alvin Plantinga and Nicholas Wolterstorff (Notre Dame: University of Notre Dame Press, 1983), 75.

17. "Religion: Modernizing the Case for God," *TIME* online, April 7, 1980, accessed February 6, 2012, http://www.time.com/time/ magazine/article/0,9171,921990-3,00.html.

18. Kelly James Clark, *Philosophers Who Believe* (Downers Grove, IL: InterVarsity Press, 1993), 10.

19. Alvin Plantinga, "Christian Philosophy at the End of the Twentieth Century," in *The Analytic Theist: An Alvin Plantinga Reader*, ed. James F. Sennett (Grand Rapids: William B. Eerdmans Publishing Company, 1998), 336.

20. Ephesians 4:22.

21. Timothy Keller, *The Reason for God: Belief in an Age of Skepticism* (New York: Riverhead Books, 2008), xvii.

PART 1: "BELIEF IN GOD IS IRRATIONAL"

Chapter 1: "Not Enough Evidence, God!"

1. Nicholas Wolterstorff, "Introduction," in *Faith and Rationality: Reason and Belief in God*, ed. Alvin Plantinga and Nicholas Wolterstorff (Notre Dame: University of Notre Dame Press, 1983), 6.

2. Ibid., 6. For details see Wolterstorff, "Can Belief in God Be Rational If It Has No Foundations?," in *Faith and Rationality: Reason and Belief in God*, ed. Alvin Plantinga and Nicholas Wolterstorff (Notre Dame: University of Notre Dame Press, 1983), 137.

3. Wolterstorff, "Introduction," 5.

4. Wolterstorff, "Can Belief in God Be Rational If It Has No Foundations?," 139.

5. Ibid., 141.

6. Wolterstorff, "Introduction," 5.

7. Ibid., 5.
8. Plantinga, "Reason and Belief in God," 24.
9. W. K. Clifford, "The Ethics of Belief," in *Philosophy of Religion: Selected Readings*, ed. William L. Rowe and William J. Wainwright (Orlando: Harcourt Brace & Company, 1998).
10. Ibid., 460.
11. Ibid. For homework, you should consider what evidence Clifford has for this claim.
12. Ibid., 461.
13. Plantinga, "Reason and Belief in God," 17–18. Also recounted in Dawkins, *The God Delusion*, 131.
14. Harris, *The End of Faith: Religion, Terror, and the Future of Reason*, 165.
15. Ibid., 17.

Chapter 2: Does Evidence Need Evidence?

1. Hitchens, *God Is Not Great: How Religion Poisons Everything*, xxii.
2. David Hume, *An Enquiry Concerning Human Understanding* (Indianapolis: Hackett Publishing Company, 1993), 30.
3. Plantinga, "Reason and Belief in God," 53.
4. Alvin Plantinga, *Warrant and Proper Function* (Oxford: Oxford University Press, 1993), 98. One common objection to this is that perhaps there *is* an inference but that it's so quick we don't notice it. There are two things to say in response to this suggestion. The first is that there's no evidence for such an inference. The second and more important thing to say is that any such inference would still require premises that don't require further inferences. That is, at some point (soon) we'd need a noninferred belief.

Chapter 3: They Should Have Seen This Coming

1. William P. Alston, "Epistemic Circularity," *Philosophy and Phenomenological Research* 47, no. 1 (1986), 5.
2. Ibid., 6–7.
3. Stenger, *The New Atheism: Taking a Stand for Science and Reason*, 60.
4. The kind of circularity we're considering here isn't circularity in the *logical* sense, in the sense that "my senses are reliable" is one of the premises of your argument. Rather it's a "practical" circularity: you assume that your senses are reliable in practice. Alston, "Epistemic Circularity," 9.

5. There's another indirect method I should mention: after considering how well all our different sense perception beliefs fit together, giving us a nice coherent view of the world, we might infer that the best explanation of this coherence is that our senses are reliable. One problem with this method—called "inference to the best explanation"—is that our understanding of what counts as the best explanation has been conditioned by our long-term assumption that our senses are reliable.

6. Plantinga, *Warrant and Proper Function*, 124.

7. Or more generally, inferring unobserved events from those we've observed.

8. Hume, *An Enquiry Concerning Human Understanding*, 27.

9. From *An Inquiry into the Human Mind,* in *Thomas Reid's Inquiry and Essays*, ed. Ronald Beanblossom and Keith Lehrer (Indianapolis: Hackett Publishing, 1983), 84–85. Quoted in Alvin Plantinga, *Warranted Christian Belief* (Oxford: Oxford University Press, 2000), 130n23.

10. Some people may wish to use the term *evidence* to refer to both arguments *and* experience. This is perfectly fine in most cases, but not when care is needed (like now).

11. This is a simpler version of Plantinga's definition of a *warranted* belief. For details on his concept of warrant and its many qualifications, see particularly his work, *Warrant and Proper Function*.

Chapter 4: Trust Me

1. Hitchens, *God Is Not Great: How Religion Poisons Everything*, 71.

2. In *De praescriptione haereticorum* (*On the prescription of heretics*).

3. Stenger, *The New Atheism: Taking a Stand for Science and Reason*, 45.

4. This of course doesn't exhaust the notion of biblical faith. Simply believing God's testimony isn't enough; our belief must result in action—in obedience, for example. In any case, we are focusing on the belief component here.

5. From Locke's *An Essay Concerning Human Understanding*, IV, 18, 2, quoted in Wolterstorff, "Can Belief in God Be Rational If It Has No Foundations?," 137.

6. For an example of the term "faith" being used in this way—as referring to the source of information—see Plantinga, "Reason and Belief in God," 89.

7. Inferences can be either deductive or inductive.
8. Philosophers sometimes add another function to our reasoning faculty, what they call *rational intuition*, which, rather than inference, is a type of experience. When you consider the proposition 2 + 1 = 3, you—as an adult at least—just *see* that it's true. Similarly, you immediately see that *modus ponens* is a valid argument form (even if you don't know it by name). I won't, however, use the term "reason" to refer to our rational intuition, but you need to know that there's a cognitive function that is sometimes included under the term "reason."
9. Plantinga, "Reason and Belief in God," 85.
10. Plantinga, *Warrant and Proper Function*, 79.
11. Ibid., 77.
12. Ibid., 79.
13. Ibid., 77.
14. From Kant's 1784 essay, "What Is Enlightenment?," http://www.english.upenn.edu/~mgamer/Etexts/kant.html.
15. Immanuel Kant, *Prolegomena to Any Future Metaphysics* (Indianapolis: Hackett Publishing Company, 1977), 5.
16. Berlinski, *The Devil's Delusion: Atheism and Its Scientific Pretensions*, 18.
17. Hume, *An Enquiry Concerning Human Understanding*, 16.
18. Thomas Reid, *An Inquiry into the Human Mind*, ed. Derek R. Brooks (University Park: Pennsylvania University Press, 1997), 4.
19. Stenger, *The New Atheism: Taking a Stand for Science and Reason*, 15.
20. N. D. Wilson, *Notes from the Tilt-a-Whirl* (book trailer) (Los Angeles: Beloved Independent, 2011).

Chapter 5: Darwin's Doubt

1. David Hume, *A Treatise of Human Nature* (Oxford: Oxford University Press, 1993), 269.
2. From *An Inquiry into the Human Mind*, in *Thomas Reid's Inquiry and Essays*, ed. Ronald Beanblossom and Keith Lehrer (Indianapolis: Hackett Publishing, 1983), 84–85. Quoted in Plantinga, *Warranted Christian Belief*, 130n23.
3. Ibid., 222.
4. Ibid., 223.
5. Ibid., 224.
6. Ibid., 225.
7. Ibid., 226.

8. Ibid.

9. One helpful difference between agnosticism (with respect to God's existence) and atheism is that the former is entirely consistent with God's existence whereas the latter isn't. That is, atheism and theism cannot both be true. A strong (principled) agnosticism that says we *can't* know whether God exists can be true even if God exists.

10. Richard Dawkins, *The Blind Watchmaker* (New York: W. W. Norton & Company, 1986), 6.

11. Ronald N. Giere, "Naturalism," in *The Routledge Companion to the Philosophy of Science*, ed. Stathis Psillos and Martin Curd (London: Routledge, 2008), 216.

12. Ibid.

13. Plantinga, *Warrant and Proper Function*, 219.

14. Eugene Wigner, "The Unreasonable Effectiveness of Mathematics in the Natural Sciences," 1960. http://www.dartmouth.edu/~matc /MathDrama/reading/Wigner.html.

15. For a host of complaints and criticisms of Plantinga's "Evolutionary Argument against Atheism" or EAAA—along with Plantinga's responses—see James Beilby, ed., *Naturalism Defeated? Essays on Plantinga's Evolutionary Argument against Naturalism* (Ithaca, NY: Cornell University Press, 2002).

16. Plantinga, *Warrant and Proper Function*, 228.

Chapter 6: Taking God for Granted

1. Plantinga, *Warranted Christian Belief*, 263.

2. Ibid., 80.

3. Ibid., 167.

4. Ibid., 175.

5. Plantinga, "Reason and Belief in God, 80. My belief that I should thank God implies that God exists to be thanked in the first place.

6. Plantinga, *Warranted Christian Belief*, 184.

7. Ibid., 177.

8. Romans 1:25.

9. Plantinga, *Warranted Christian Belief*, 185.

10. Of course, there are additional explanations. For one thing, philosophy is hard.

11. Thomas Nagel, *The Last Word* (Oxford: Oxford University Press, 1997), 130.

12. Christopher Hitchens, *The Portable Atheist: Essential Readings for the Nonbeliever*, xxii.

13. Plantinga, *Warranted Christian Belief*, 180.

14. Ibid., 243.

15. Although the term is the best I can come up with, I also use it out of habit, a habit too ingrained to change now.

Chapter 7: "Aw, Come On!" (Some Objections)

1. In Peter Devries's *Mackerel Plaza*, Mackerel says, "It is the final proof of God's existence that he need not exist in order to save us."

2. Plantinga, *Warranted Christian Belief*, 352.

3. If you're curious, the full argument is (1) If the Christian epistemic story is true, then belief in God can be rational apart from any evidence; (2) the Christian epistemic story is true; (3) therefore belief in God can be rational apart from any evidence. If the second premise is false, we can't infer that the conclusion is false. All we can say is that our argument isn't any good. There may be other arguments—good ones—for the conclusion.

4. Plantinga, *Warranted Christian Belief*, 191.

5. Ibid., 343–44.

6. Harris, *The End of Faith: Religion, Terror, and the Future of Reason*, 223.

7. Penn Jillette, "There Is No God," in *The Portable Atheist: Essential Readings for the Nonbeliever*, ed. Christopher Hitchens (Cambridge, MA: Da Capo Press, 2007), 350.

8. Plantinga, *Warranted Christian Belief*, 343.

9. In fact, nearly any belief is possibly subject to defeat. Plantinga, *Warrant and Proper Function*, 41.

10. Plantinga, "Reason and Belief in God," 74.

11. Ibid., 78.

INTERMISSION: THE ART OF SELF-DEFENSE

Chapter 8: Let's Be Realistic

1. Plantinga, *Warranted Christian Belief*, 170.

2. The law of the excluded middle says that a declarative statement is either true or false.

3. Thankfully, this paper has finally been published as an appendix in

Alvin Plantinga, ed. Deane-Peter Baker, Contemporary Philosophy in Focus (Cambridge: Cambridge University Press, 2007).

4. Ibid., 210.

5. Ibid. When it comes to arguments in science, Thomas Kuhn says, "Because scientists are reasonable men, one or another argument will ultimately persuade many of them. But there is no single argument that can or should persuade them all." Thomas S. Kuhn, *The Structure of Scientific Revolutions*, 3d ed. (Chicago: University of Chicago Press, 1996), 158.

6. Keller, *The Reason for God: Belief in an Age of Skepticism*, 131ff.

7. Stephen Hawking and Leonard Mlodinow, *The Grand Design* (New York: Bantam Books, 2010), 128. Emphasis added.

8. William E. Carroll, "Galileo and the Inquisition I," International Catholic University, accessed February 6, 2012, http://home.comcast.net/~icuweb/c02905.htm.

9. Kuhn, *The Structure of Scientific Revolutions*, 85.

10. Ibid., 78.

11. Ibid., 113.

12. Ibid., 112.

13. Ibid., 126–27.

14. Ibid., 116.

15. Harris, *The End of Faith: Religion, Terror, and the Future of Reason*, 75.

16. Kuhn, *The Structure of Scientific Revolutions*, 151.

17. Ibid., 122.

18. Ibid., 151.

19. Ibid., 136.

20. Keller, *The Reason for God: Belief in an Age of Skepticism*, 53.

21. "The Last Word," 130, from Keller's *The Reason for God*, 123.

22. For a helpful discussion of the limits of philosophical arguments—of which the argument for God's existence is included—see Peter van Inwagen's 2003 Gifford Lectures, particularly the lecture on "philosophical failure." Peter van Inwagen, *The Problem of Evil: The Gifford Lectures Delivered in the University of St Andrews in 2003* (Oxford: Clarendon Press, 2006).

Chapter 9: Starting an Argument

1. Plantinga, *Warranted Christian Belief*, 358.

2. *Politics*, 1303b30. Aristotle is quoting an ancient proverb.

3. Plantinga, "Reason and Belief in God," 25.

4. Ibid., 27.

5. See Plantinga's extended discussion for more problems with Scriven's position. Ibid., 27ff.

6. Harris, *The End of Faith: Religion, Terror, and the Future of Reason*, 46–47.

7. Dawkins, *The God Delusion*, 77.

8. Daniel C. Dennett and Alvin Plantinga, *Science and Religion: Are They Compatible?*, ed. James P. Sterba, Point/Counterpoint Series (Oxford: Oxford University Press, 2010), 28.

Chapter 10: Law and Order

1. I should add that we are indebted to Kant for the current terminology of theistic arguments. It is from Kant that we learned to call the three major class of arguments the *teleological, cosmological,* and *ontological* arguments.

2. Similarly, Wittgenstein's influence outside of philosophy is inversely proportional to his clarity.

3. Immanuel Kant, *Critique of Practical Reason* (Indianapolis: Hackett Publishing Company, 2002), 203.

4. Psalm 19:1–4.

5. Matthew 11:17.

6. Romans 2:14–15.

PART 2: "SCIENCE HAS SHOWN THERE'S NO GOD"

Chapter 11: Galileo and the Needless War

1. Hal Boedeker, posted by halboedeker on June 7, 2010, 10:42 a.m., "Stephen Hawking tells Diane Sawyer: Science will win over religion," *Orlando Sentinel*, accessed February 6, 2012, http://blogs.orlandosentinel.com/entertainment_tv_tvblog/2010/06/stephen-hawking-tells-diane-sawyer-science-will-win-over-religion.html.

2. Keller, *The Reason for God: Belief in an Age of Skepticism*, 92. Keller's source is Edward Larson and Larry Witham's article, "Scientists Are Still Keeping the Faith," *Nature* 386/:435–36. (April 3, 1997).

3. Ronald L. Numbers, "Aggressors, Victims, and Peacemakers: Historical Actors in the Drama of Science and Religion," in *The*

Religion and Science Debate: Why Does It Continue?, ed. Harold
W. Attridge (New Haven, CT: Yale University Press, 2009), 47.
Numbers is a former Seventh-day Adventist who "lost his religious
faith." (See http://www.salon.com/books/int/2007/01/02/numbers.)
4. Victor J. Stenger, *God: The Failed Hypothesis—How Science Shows That
God Does Not Exist* (Amherst, NY: Prometheus Books, 2008), 28.
5. Dawkins, *The God Delusion*, 78.
6. Stenger, *The New Atheism: Taking a Stand for Science and Reason*, 74.
7. Dawkins, *The God Delusion*, 78.
8. Numbers, "Aggressors, Victims, and Peacemakers: Historical Actors in
the Drama of Science and Religion," 49.
9. David C. Lindberg and Ronald L. Numbers, eds., *God & Nature:
Historical Essays on the Encounter between Christianity and Science*
(Berkeley: University of California Press,1986), 1.
10. Stenger, *The New Atheism: Taking a Stand for Science and Reason*, 73.
11. Numbers, "Aggressors, Victims, and Peacemakers: Historical Actors in
the Drama of Science and Religion," 33.
12. Ibid.
13. Maurice A. Finocchiaro, *The Galileo Affair: A Documentary History*
(Berkeley: University of California Press, 1989), 135.
14. Thomas Dixon, *Science and Religion: A Very Short Introduction* (Oxford:
Oxford University Press, 2008), 18.
15. From his 1613 letter to Castelli, reprinted in Maurice A. Finocchiaro,
The Essential Galileo (Indianapolis: Hackett Publishing Company,
1989), 104.
16. Ibid.
17. Ibid., 106.
18. From his *Dialogue Concerning the Two Chief World Systems* (New York:
The Modern Library, 2001), 381.
19. Mitch Stokes, *Galileo* (Nashville: Thomas Nelson, 2011), 157.
20. Finocchiaro, *The Essential Galileo*, 137–38.
21. Ibid., 114.
22. Ibid., 147.
23. Stokes, *Galileo*, 133.
24. James Reston Jr., *Galileo: A Life* (Washington, DC: Beard Books, 2000),
237.
25. Hawking and Mlodinow, *The Grand Design*, 41.

26. William R. Shea and Mariano Artigas, *Galileo in Rome: The Rise and Fall of a Troublesome Genius* (Oxford: Oxford University Press, 2003), 195.

27. Stillman Drake, *Galileo: A Very Short Introduction* (Oxford: Oxford University Press, 2001), 116.

28. Ibid., 117.

29. Stokes, *Galileo*, 130.

30. Dawkins, *The God Delusion*, 124.

31. Stenger, *The New Atheism: Taking a Stand for Science and Reason*, 73.

32. Dawkins, *The God Delusion*, 123.

33. Hitchens, ed., *The Portable Atheist: Essential Readings for the Nonbeliever*, xxi.

Chapter 12: The Lazy God

1. Hitchens, *God Is Not Great: How Religion Poisons Everything*, 66.

2. Morris Kline, *Mathematics and the Physical World* (New York: Thomas Y. Crowell Company, 1959), 419–20.

3. Morris Kline, *Mathematics: The Loss of Certainty* (Oxford: Oxford University Press, 1980), 73.

4. Emphasis is Hitchens's. Hitchens, *God Is Not Great: How Religion Poisons Everything*, 67.

5. Causes aren't the only kinds of explanations. If I ask *Why did you hit me?* or *Why does God allow suffering and evil?*, I'm not necessarily asking for a cause. But I do want to understand a fact I'm already convinced of, namely, that you hit me or that there is evil and suffering in the world.

6. Brewster, D. (2005 [1855]). *Memoirs of the Life, Writings, and Discoveries of Sir Isaac Newton; Vol. 2*, Adamant Media Corporation, 392.

7. Hitchens, *God Is Not Great: How Religion Poisons Everything*, 66.

8. Kline, *Mathematics and the Physical World*, 420.

9. Dawkins, *The God Delusion*, 151.

10. Sam Harris, *Letter to a Christian Nation* (New York: Vintage Books, 2006), 107.

11. Dawkins, *The God Delusion*, 144.

12. Hitchens, *God Is Not Great: How Religion Poisons Everything*, 282.

13. Alvin Plantinga, "Methodological Naturalism? Part 2," *Origins & Design* 18, no. 2 (1997), http://www.arn.org/docs/odesign/od182/methnat182.htm.

14. Ibid.

15. Dawkins, *The God Delusion*, 83.
16. Plantinga, "Methodological Naturalism? Part 2."
17. Ibid.

Chapter 13: There's No Need to Explain

1. Berlinski, *The Devil's Delusion: Atheism and Its Scientific Pretensions*, 109.
2. Neil A. Manson, ed., *God and Design: The Teleological Argument and Modern Science* (London: Routledge, 2003), 4.
3. Dawkins, *The God Delusion*, 172.
4. Ibid.
5. Ibid., 173.
6. Peter van Inwagen, *Metaphysics*, ed. Norman Daniels and Keith Lehrer, 2d ed., Dimensions of Philosophy Series (Boulder: Westview Press, 2002), 151.
7. Alvin Plantinga, "Methodological Naturalism? Part 1," *Origins & Design* 18, no. 1 (1997), http://www.arn.org/docs/odesign/od181/methnat181.htm.
8. Berlinski, *The Devil's Delusion: Atheism and Its Scientific Pretensions*, xii.

Chapter 14: 100% All Natural?

1. Plantinga, "Methodological Naturalism? Part 2."
2. Paul Davies, "Design in Physics and Cosmology," in *God and Design: The Teleological Argument and Modern Science*, ed. Neil A. Manson (London: Routledge, 2003), 148.
3. Stenger, *The New Atheism: Taking a Stand for Science and Reason*, 71.
4. Eugene Wigner, "The Unreasonable Effectiveness of Mathematics in the Natural Sciences," http://www.dartmouth.edu/~matc/MathDrama/reading/Wigner.html. Wigner's article originally appeared in *Communications in Pure and Applied Mathematics*, 13, no. 1 (February 1960).
5. Albert Einstein, "Physics and Reality," in *Out of My Later Years* (New York: Citadel Press, 1984), 61.
6. Stenger, *The New Atheism: Taking a Stand for Science and Reason*, 71.
7. Kuhn, *The Structure of Scientific Revolutions*, 173.
8. Plantinga, "Methodological Naturalism? Part 1."
9. Ibid.
10. Ibid.

11. That is, we learned that "old beliefs control new beliefs" in chapter 8.
12. Plantinga, "Methodological Naturalism? Part 1."
13. Ibid.
14. Plantinga, "Methodological Naturalism? Part 2."
15. The following statement is from Judge Jones's memorandum opinion on the 2005 *Kitzmiller v. Dover Area School District* case: "This rigorous attachment to 'natural' explanations is an essential attribute to science by definition and by convention. We are in agreement with Plaintiffs' lead expert Dr. Miller, that from a practical perspective, attributing unsolved problems about nature to causes and forces that lie outside the natural world is a 'science stopper.' As Dr. Miller explained, once you attribute a cause to an untestable supernatural force, a proposition that cannot be disproven, there is no reason to continue seeking natural explanations as we have our answer." http://www.ucs.louisiana.edu/~ras2777/relpol/kitzmiller.htm.
16. Plantinga, "Methodological Naturalism? Part 2."
17. Plantinga, "Methodological Naturalism? Part 1."
18. Ibid.
19. Ibid.

Chapter 15: Looking for God

1. Berlinski, *The Devil's Delusion: Atheism and Its Scientific Pretensions*, xiii–xiv.
2. Hawking and Mlodinow, *The Grand Design*, 41–42.
3. Stenger, *God: The Failed Hypothesis—How Science Shows That God Does Not Exist*, 27.
4. Stenger, *The New Atheism: Taking a Stand for Science and Reason*, 81–82.
5. Stenger, *God: The Failed Hypothesis*, 262.

Chapter 16: Evolution Explained?

1. Interview with Gary Habermas http://www.biola.edu/antonyflew/flew-interview.pdf.
2. Giere, "Naturalism," 215.
3. Stenger, *God: The Failed Hypothesis*, 61.
4. Ibid., 63.
5. Ibid., 64.
6. Dawkins, *The God Delusion*, 141.
7. Keith Thomson, "Introduction," in *The Religion and Science Debate:*

Why Does It Continue?, ed. Harold W. Attridge (New Haven, CT: Yale University Press, 2009), 11.

8. "Letter from Darwin to Hooker," *The Life and Letters of Charles Darwin*, vol. 2, ed. Francis Darwin (New York: Appleton, 1967), 202. From Plantinga, "Methodological Naturalism? Part 1."

9. Dawkins, *The God Delusion*, 162.

10. Jane Gregory, *Fred Hoyle's Universe* (Oxford: Oxford University Press, 2005), 296.

11. Ibid., 297.

12. Hitchens, *God Is Not Great: How Religion Poisons Everything*, 86.

13. Plantinga, "Methodological Naturalism? Part 1."

14. Dawkins, *The God Delusion*, 103.

Chapter 17: The User-Friendly Universe

1. From *The Assayer* (1623), reprinted in Finocchiaro, *The Essential Galileo*, 183.

2. Mark Steiner, *The Applicability of Mathematics as a Philosophical Problem* (Cambridge, MA: Harvard University Press, 1998), 14.

3. Albert Einstein, "Geometry and Experience," in *Sidelights on Relativity* (Mineola, NY: Dover), 12.

4. Steiner, *The Applicability of Mathematics as a Philosophical Problem*, 13.

5. Ibid., 14.

6. Wigner, "The Unreasonable Effectiveness of Mathematics in the Natural Sciences."

7. Morris Kline, *Mathematics in Western Culture* (Oxford: Oxford University Press, 1953), 78.

8. Wigner, "The Unreasonable Effectiveness of Mathematics in the Natural Sciences."

9. Ibid.

10. Steiner, *The Applicability of Mathematics as a Philosophical Problem*, 6.

11. Ibid., 48.

12. Ibid., 136.

13. Ibid., 156ff.

14. Ibid., 83.

15. Ibid., 82.

16. Ibid., 83.

17. Ibid.

18. Ibid., 6.

19. "But mathematicians do not regard theorems about this specific structure as worth bothering about." Ibid., 6.
20. Ibid., 65.
21. Wigner, "The Unreasonable Effectiveness of Mathematics in the Natural Sciences."
22. Steiner, *The Applicability of Mathematics as a Philosophical Problem*, 64.
23. Although it is probably only a one-to-one correspondence—a type of matching—that's needed.
24. Dawkins, *The God Delusion*, 412.
25. Wigner, "The Unreasonable Effectiveness of Mathematics in the Natural Sciences." For example, complex numbers, Hilbert spaces, and the abstract classification scheme SU(3), which was used to predict the existence—and discovery—of quarks.
26. Stenger, *The New Atheism: Taking a Stand for Science and Reason*, 77.

Chapter 18: The Reluctant Supernaturalist

1. W. V. Quine, "Mr. Strawson on Logical Theory" in *The Ways of Paradox* (Cambridge, MA: Harvard University Press, 1976), 151.
2. W. V. Quine, *Quine in Dialogue* (Cambridge, MA: Harvard University Press), ed. Dagfinn Follesdal and Douglas B. Quine, 27.
3. Quine's own project of "naturalizing philosophy" used "naturalizing" in a somewhat different sense.
4. Peter van Inwagen, "A Theory of Properties," in *Oxford Studies in Metaphysics, Volume 1*, ed. Dean W. Zimmerman (Oxford: Oxford University Press, 2004), 107.
5. Ibid., 113.
6. For the curious reader, here's what such a paraphrase might look like. "Santa is fat" becomes, by the logician's alchemy, "Each thing is such that if it is Santa then it is fat" or more cryptically, "For every object, x, if x is Santa then x is fat." This works because of the "if" in the sentence. In the notation of quantificational logic we can express the original sentence this way: "$\forall x(Sx \supset Fx)$." This sentence turns out true because the antecedent of the conditional (the "if" part) is false, which makes the conditional (the entire "if-then" statement) true. This sentence doesn't refer specifically to Santa but rather to any object that you happen to select out of all existing objects. By the original sentence, we're really just referring to all existing objects and saying, that if one of them happened to be Santa, it would be fat.

None of them *would* happen to be Santa of course, but if it did turn out to be Santa, we know that it would be fat.

7. And so Quine's argument for the existence of mathematical objects is called the "Indispensability Argument."

8. Stenger, *The New Atheism: Taking a Stand for Science and Reason,* 21–22.

9. Alvin Plantinga, *Does God Have a Nature?* (Milwaukee: Marquette University Press, 1980), 142–43.

10. Ibid., 4–5.

11. Ibid., 5.

12. Ibid., 144.

PART 3: "EVIL AND SUFFERING SHOW THERE'S NO GOD"

Chapter 19: Ye Olde Problem of Evil

1. Michael Ruse, *Evolution and Religion: A Dialogue* (Lanham: Rowman & Littlfield Publishers, 2008), 64.

2. David Hume, *Dialogues Concerning Natural Religion* (Indianapolis: Hackett, 1998), 63.

3. Plantinga, *Warranted Christian Belief,* 460.

4. Plantinga, *God and Other Minds: A Study of the Rational Justification of Belief in God* (Ithaca, NY: Cornell University Press, 1967), 132.

5. Plantinga, "Reason and Belief in God," 21.

6. Plantinga, *Warranted Christian Belief,* 462.

7. Alvin Plantinga, *God, Freedom, and Evil* (Grand Rapids, MI: William B. Eerdmans Publishing Co., 1974), 61.

8. Plantinga, *Warranted Christian Belief,* 464.

9. Of course, in real life, we're never given *merely* the fact of evil—or anything else; we always have a whole host of beliefs at any given moment that come to bear on any question of what further we should believe.

10. Plantinga, *Warranted Christian Belief,* 465–66.

11. Ibid., 466.

12. Keller, *The Reason for God: Belief in an Age of Skepticism,* 25.

13. Plantinga, *Warranted Christian Belief,* 497.

14. Keller, *The Reason for God: Belief in an Age of Skepticism,* 24.

15. Plantinga, *Warranted Christian Belief,* 483.

16. Ibid., 488.
17. Ibid.
18. Ibid., 489.
19. Ibid.

Chapter 20: The Atheist's Problem (of Evil)

1. Daniel C. Dennett, *Darwin's Dangerous Idea: Evolution and the Meanings of Life* (New York: Simon & Schuster, 1995), 515.
2. Ibid., 516.
3. Hitchens, *God Is Not Great: How Religion Poisons Everything*.
4. Darren Doane, *Collision* (Level 4, 2009) (documentary).
5. Hitchens, *God Is Not Great: How Religion Poisons Everything*, 18.
6. Stenger scoffs, "Many of the theist books critical of New Atheism attempt to argue that 'atheists' like Hitler and Stalin killed more people than all the kings of Christendom, the Crusades, and the Inquisition put together." Stenger, *The New Atheism: Taking a Stand for Science and Reason*, 241.
7. Dawkins, *The God Delusion*, 411.
8. Marc Hauser and Peter Singer, "Morality without Religion," http://www.wjh.harvard.edu/~mnkylab/publications/recent/HauserSingerMoralRelig05.pdf.
9. Ibid.
10. Harris, *The End of Faith: Religion, Terror, and the Future of Reason*, 226.
11. Samir Okasha, *Philosophy of Science: A Very Short Introduction* (Oxford: Oxford University Press, 2002), 131–32.
12. Ibid., 133.
13. http://www.peta.org/about/why-peta/why-animal-rights.aspx.
14. Stenger, *The New Atheism: Taking a Stand for Science and Reason*, 14.
15. Dawkins, *The God Delusion*, 81.
16. Christopher Hitchens; "Message to American Atheists," http://richarddawkins.net/articles/618232-message-to-american-atheists. Stenger, too, thinks something similar: "Furthermore, we do not see morality as god-given but rather the result of humanity's own social development." Stenger, *The New Atheism: Taking a Stand for Science and Reason*, 14.
17. Harris, *The End of Faith: Religion, Terror, and the Future of Reason*, 226.
18. Stenger, *The New Atheism: Taking a Stand for Science and Reason*, 221.
19. Marc Hauser and Peter Singer, "Morality without Religion," http://

www.wjh.harvard.edu/~mnkylab/publications/recent
/HauserSingerMoralRelig05.pdf.

20. Hitchens, ed., *The Portable Atheist: Essential Readings for the Nonbeliever*, xvii.

21. Stenger, *The New Atheism: Taking a Stand for Science and Reason*, 69–70.

22. Quoted in Stenger, *God: The Failed Hypothesis*, 71.

23. Alvin Plantinga, "A Christian Life Partly Lived," in *Philosophers Who Believe: The Spiritual Journeys of 11 Leading Thinkers*, ed. Kelly James Clark (Downers Grove, IL: InterVarsity Press, 1993), 73.

24. Ibid., 73. That is, (1) If evil exists, then God exists; (2) Evil exists; (3) Therefore God exists. The atheists' argument associated with the traditional problem of evil, on the other hand, is (1) If evil exists, then God (probably) doesn't exist; (2) Evil exists; (3) Therefore God (probably) doesn't exist. The "probably" is added in the case of the probabilistic problem of evil; it can be removed for the logical problem of evil.

25. C. S. Lewis, *Mere Christianity* (Westwood, NJ: Barbour and Company, Inc., 1952), 33–34. Recall the atheist's challenge: (1) If evil exists, then God (probably) doesn't exist; (2) Evil exists; (3) Therefore God (probably) doesn't exist. But if there's no evil, premise (2) is false and the argument fails. Of course, this failure doesn't imply that God *does* exist, but merely that this particular argument fails to show that he doesn't. If, however, this argument is the only thing preventing a person from believing in God (as Lewis seems to imply about his own situation), the failure of the argument may be enough to open the door to belief in God.

26. Hitchens, ed. *The Portable Atheist: Essential Readings for the Nonbeliever*, xxi.

27. Ibid., xvi.

28. Stenger, *The New Atheism: Taking a Stand for Science and Reason*, 150.

29. That is, the atheist's argument is (1) If God commands rape, then rape is good; (2) God commands rape; (3) Therefore rape is good. But if what we've said about the necessity of God's character is right, then the second premise could *never* be true—it's necessarily false.

Chapter 21: Conclusion: Damaged Goods

1. Plantinga, *Warrant and Proper Function*, 195.
2. Ibid., 198.
3. Ibid., 200.
4. Harris, *The End of Faith: Religion, Terror, and the Future of Reason*, 226.
5. But that's not all. Plantinga has argued that it is very difficult to even make sense of the notion of "belief" on a naturalistic worldview. If he's right, then the problem for the atheist just gets worse.

INDEX

Dixon, Thomas, 105
doubts, vii, xvii
  absence of reason for, 51
Drake, Stillman, 110
Draper, John William, *History of the Conflict Between Science and Religion*, 103
Dyson, Freeman, 125
earth-centered universe, vs. sun-centered, 76
earth, stationary vs. moving, 106
Edwards, Jonathan, 50
Einstein, Albert, 77–78, 135, 163
elements, 126
End of Faith, The (Harris), ix–x
Enlightenment, 3, 19, 26, 33, 34, 64, 159, 161–63, 172
  and rejection of tradition, 37, 209–10
  and Scientific Revolution, 173
enthusiasts, 5
ethical standards, evolutionary theory and, 212
Euthyphro (Plato), 215
evidence, vii, 226ch3n10
  belief in God separate from, 63
  for God, 3–9, 11–17, 148
evidentialism, 5, 9, 14, 64, 73, 94
  congenital, 7–9
  evaluating, 16
  as problem, 15–16
evil, 189–201, 213. *See also* suffering
  atheist argument for no reason for allowing, 195
  atheists and, 220
  God and, 191
evolution, 48, 137–38, 140, 141, 151–58, 170, 207
  ethical standards and, 211–12
  God's existence and, 156
  as hypothesis, 114
  of organisms, 152
  Stenger on, 153
  survival as goal, 43
excluded middle, law of, 229ch8n2
experience
  as basis for beliefs, 30
  as input, 24–25
explanations, 13, 121, 124–25
external objects, belief in existence of, 23
faith, 31, 38, 159, 226ch4n6
  of Abraham, 31
  and beliefs, 47
  contexts for, 31
  foolishness of, x
  need for discrimination, 49
  without doubts, xvii

Feynman, Richard, 163
Flew, Antony, 89, 151
Forms of Plato, 176–78, 179–80, 184
  as divine ideas, 185
foundational beliefs, 14, 17
free will, 192–93, 197
freedom of speech, xii
French Revolution, 4, 36
Freud, Sigmund, 89
future, past and, 21–22
Galileo, 7, 77, 103–4, 105, 125–26, 160
  denial of senses, 106–7
  Dialogue Concerning the Two Chief World Systems, 109
  Letter to the Grand Duchess Christina, 107–8
  loyalty to the church, 110
geocentricity, 76
Giere, Ronald, 43, 152
God, xiv, 221
  absurdity of belief, x
  Bible as God speaking to us, 51
  conflict between science and belief in, vii
  as divine lawgiver, 212–14
  and existence of evil, 191
  humans as creation, 55, 198–200
  indifference to existence, 83
  intellect of, 195–96
  involvement, 119
  looking for, 143–50
  mathematics and existence of, 173
  objects not created by, 184–85
  observation or theory, 147–48
  physical clues for existence, 151
  science caring about, 140–41
  as science stopper, 139–40
  spoken world, 159–61
  as standard, 215–16
  and suffering, 197, 199
  as superfluous, 113
  taking for granted, 49–59
  unchangeable character, 216
God Delusion, The (Dawkins), 155
God hypothesis, 115–16
God-of-the-gaps explanation, 116–18, 121
  problem with, 118, 120
God: The Failed Hypothesis (Stenger), 143
Golden Rule, 211
"Goldilocks zone," 124
gospel, belief in, 58
Gould, Stephen Jay, 102, 128
Grand Evolutionary Myth, 144, 207
gravity, 127

ABOUT THE AUTHOR

Mitch Stokes is a Senior Fellow of Philosophy at New St. Andrews College in Moscow, Idaho. He received his PhD in philosophy from Notre Dame under the direction of Alvin Plantinga and Peter van Inwagen. At Yale, he earned an MA in religion under the direction of Nicholas Wolterstorff. He also holds an MS in mechanical engineering and, prior to his philosophy career, worked for an international engineering firm where he earned five patents in aeroderivative gas turbine technology. He and his wife, Christine, have four children—and a bulldog named Roscoe.

MORE FROM MITCH STOKES

Christian Encounters, a series of biographies from Thomas Nelson Publishers, highlights important lives from all ages and areas of the Church. Some are familiar faces. Others are unexpected guests. But all, through their relationships, struggles, prayers, and desires, uniquely illuminate our shared experience.

As an inventor, astronomer, physicist, and philosopher, Isaac Newton forever changed the way we see and understand the world. Surprisingly, he wrote more about faith and religion than on all these subjects combined. Because of his diligence in both scientific and biblical study, Newton had a tremendous impact on religious thought that is still evident today.

It's no mystery how profound a role Galileo played in the Scientific Revolution. Less explored is the Italian innovator's sincere, guiding faith in God. In this exhaustively researched biography that reads like a page-turning novel, Mitch Stokes draws on his expertise in philosophy, logic, math, and science to attune modern ears with Galileo's controversial genius.

Available wherever books and ebooks are sold